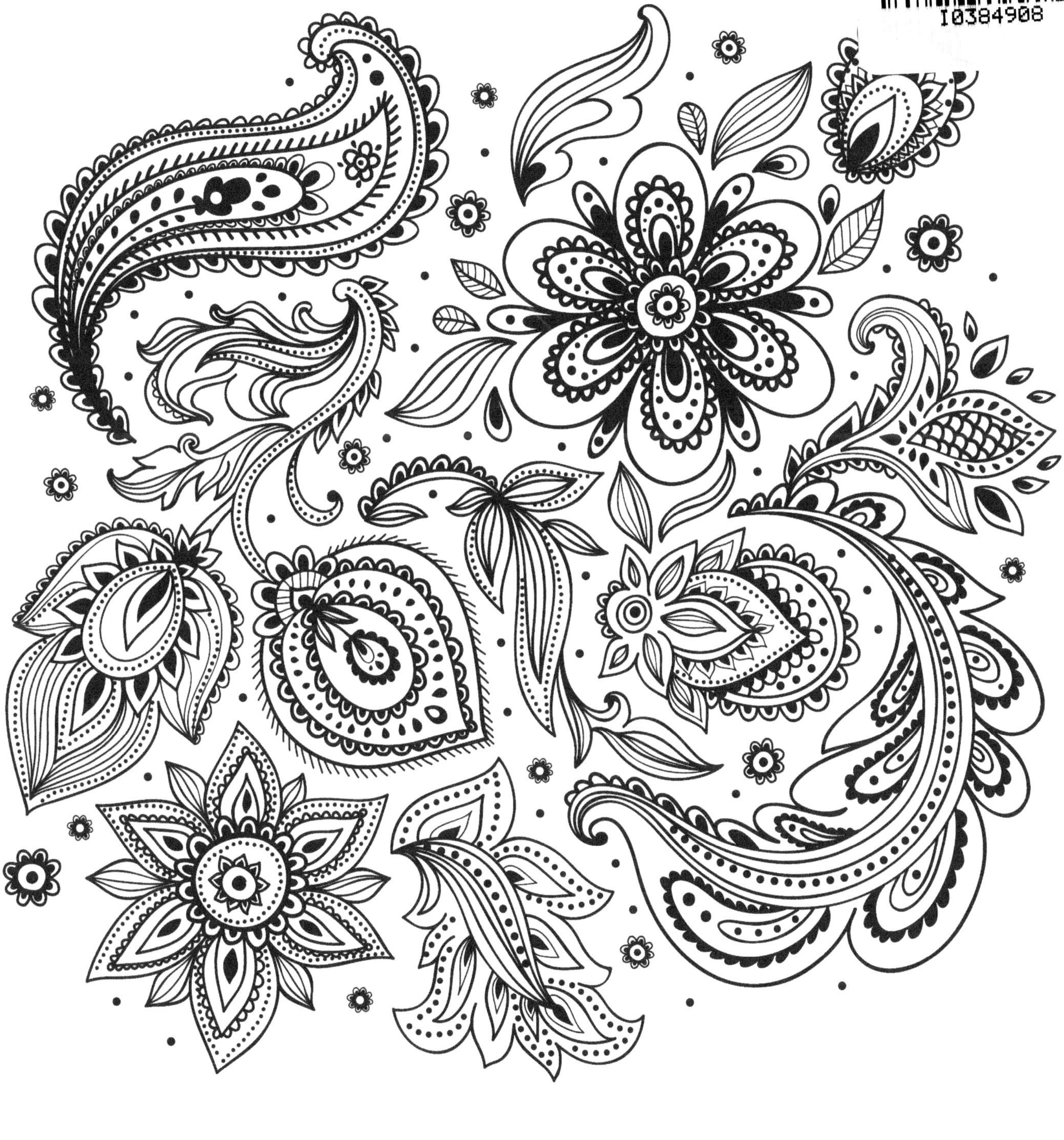

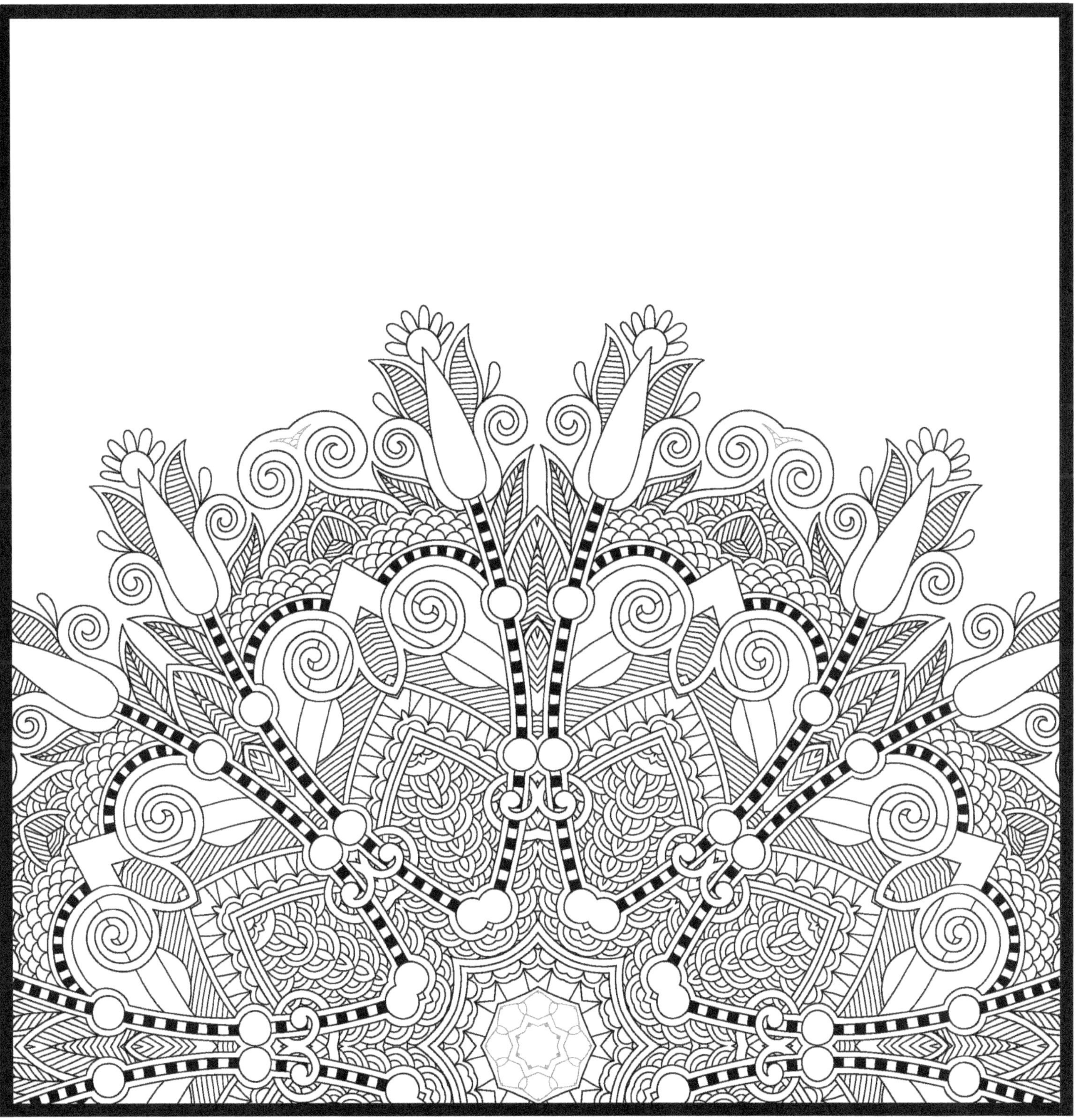

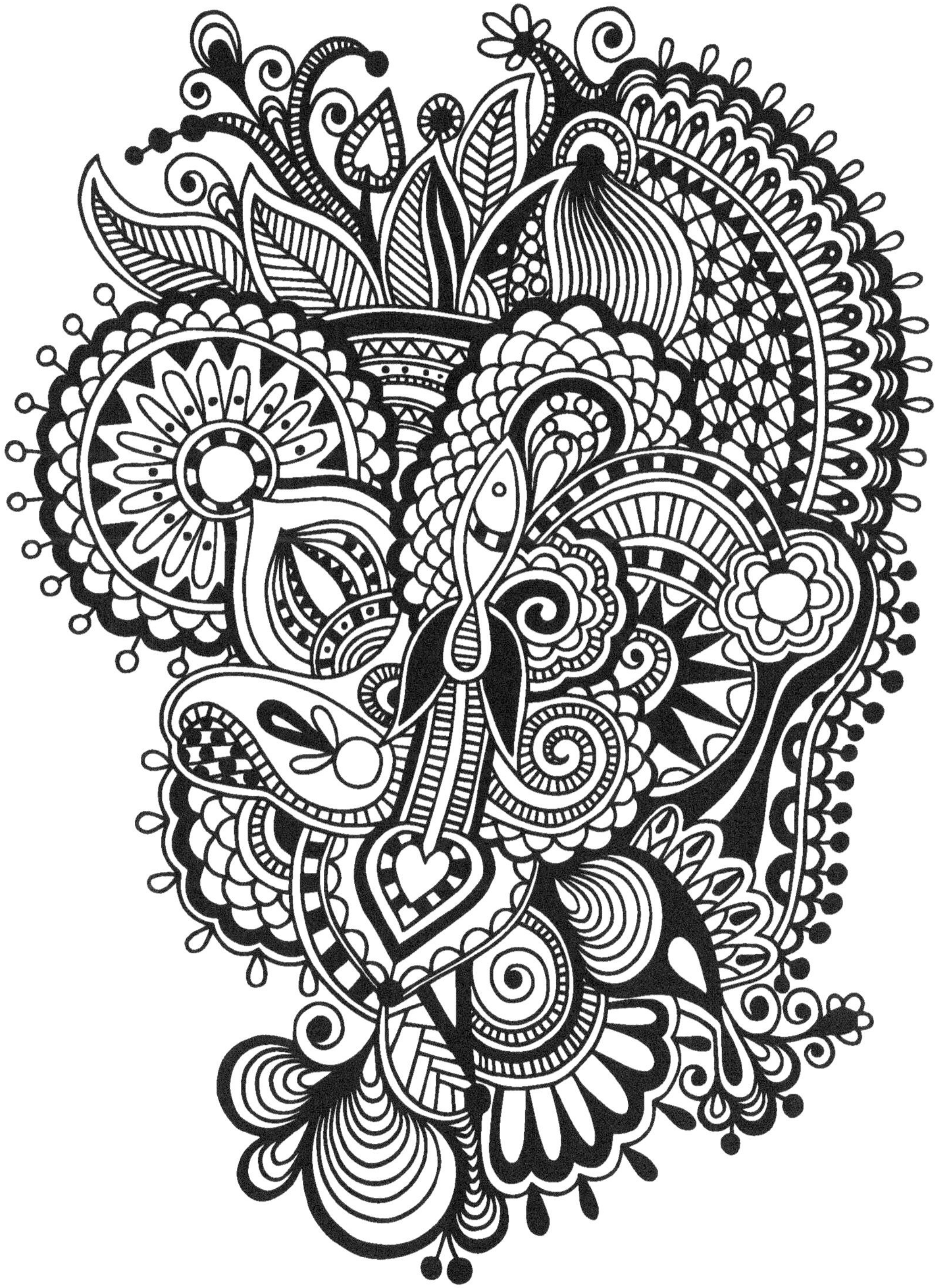

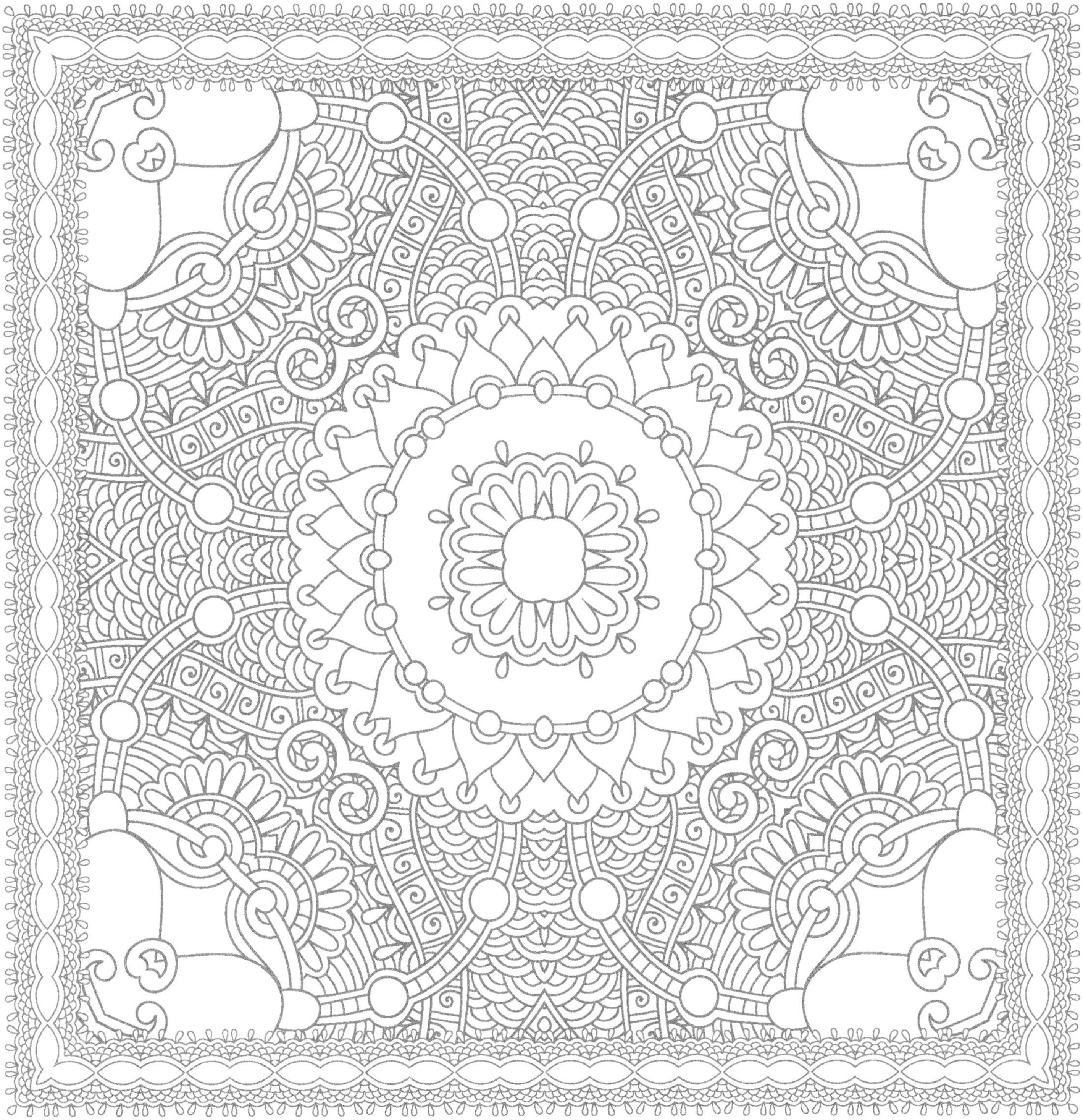

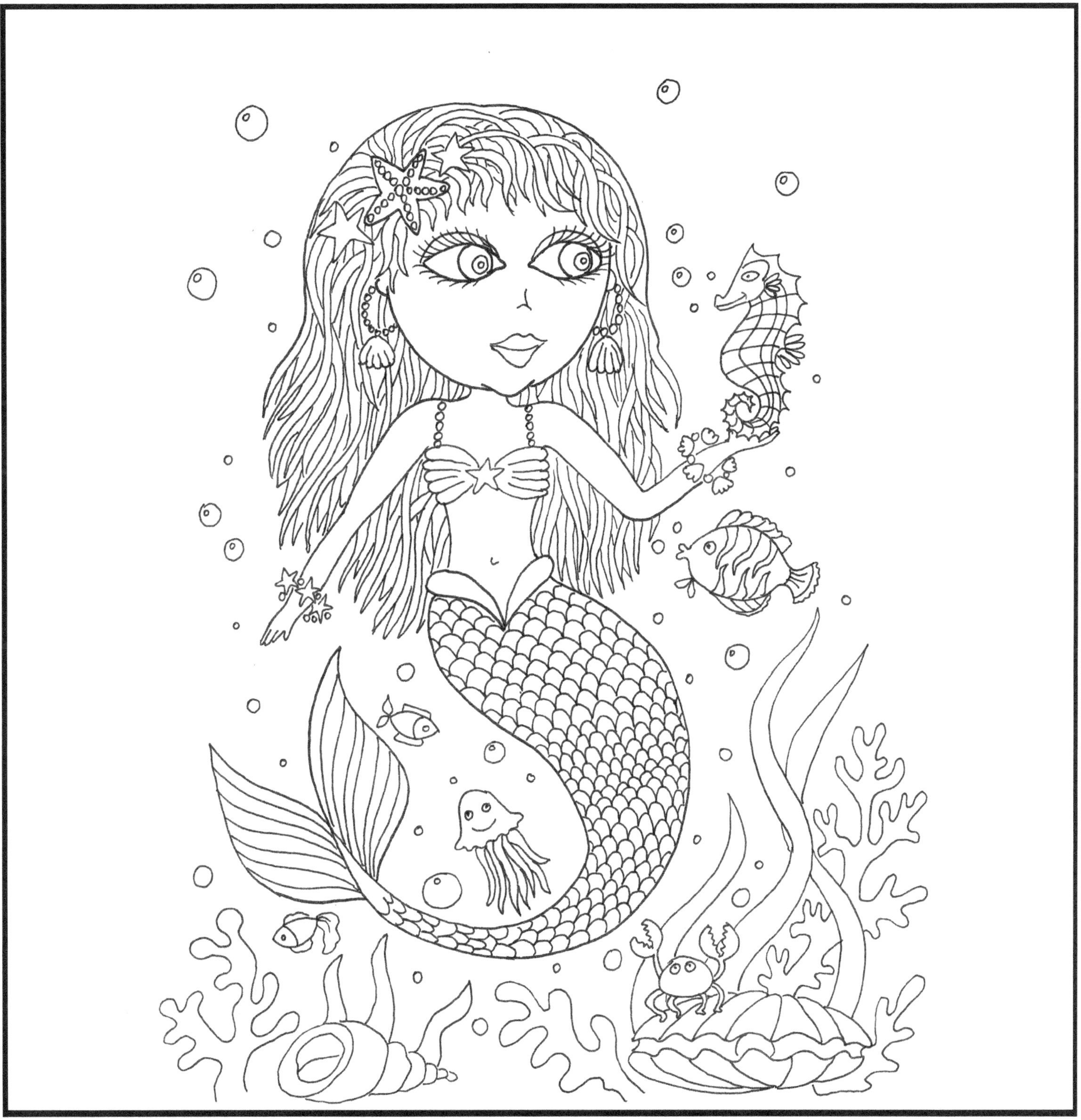

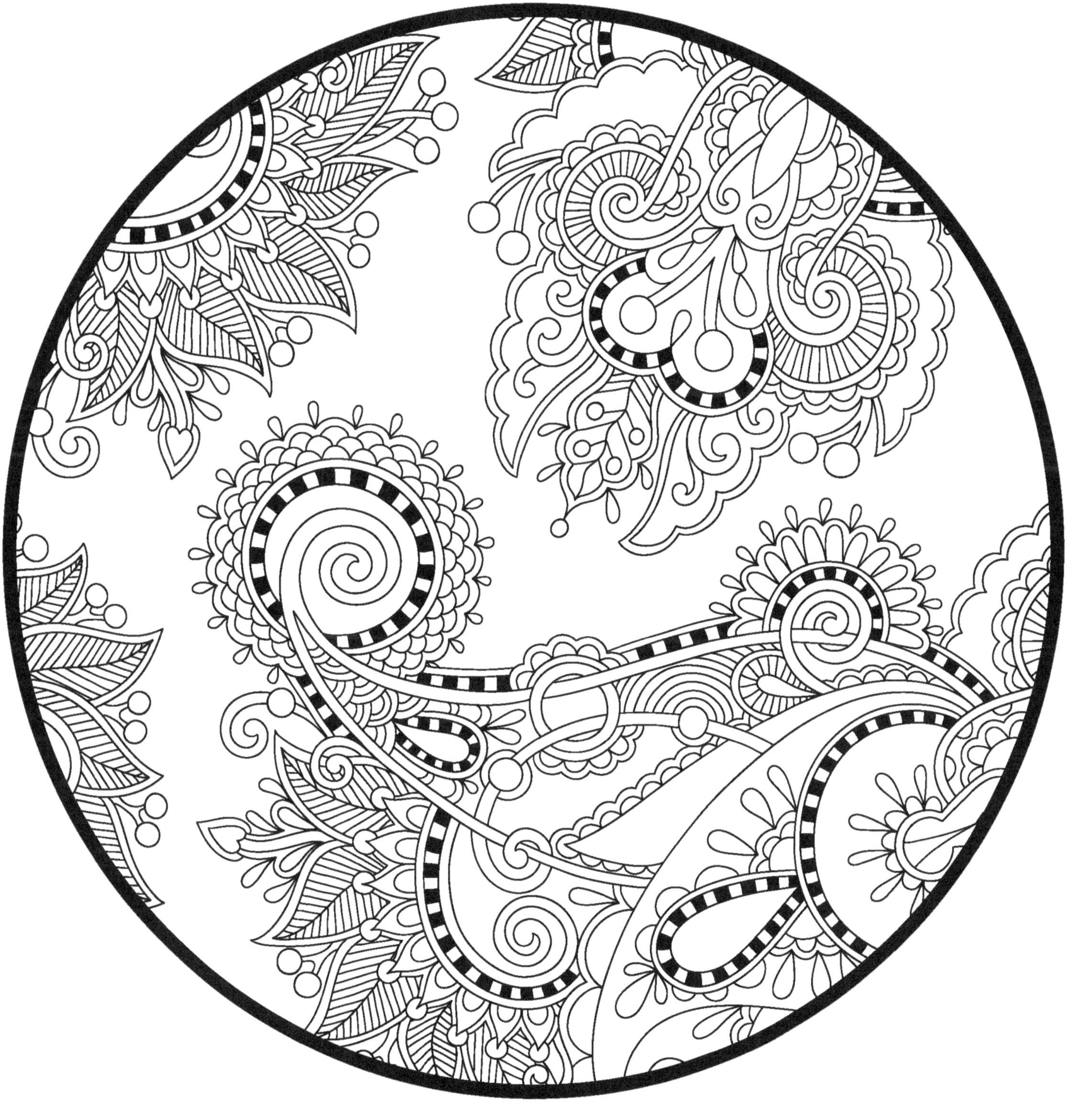

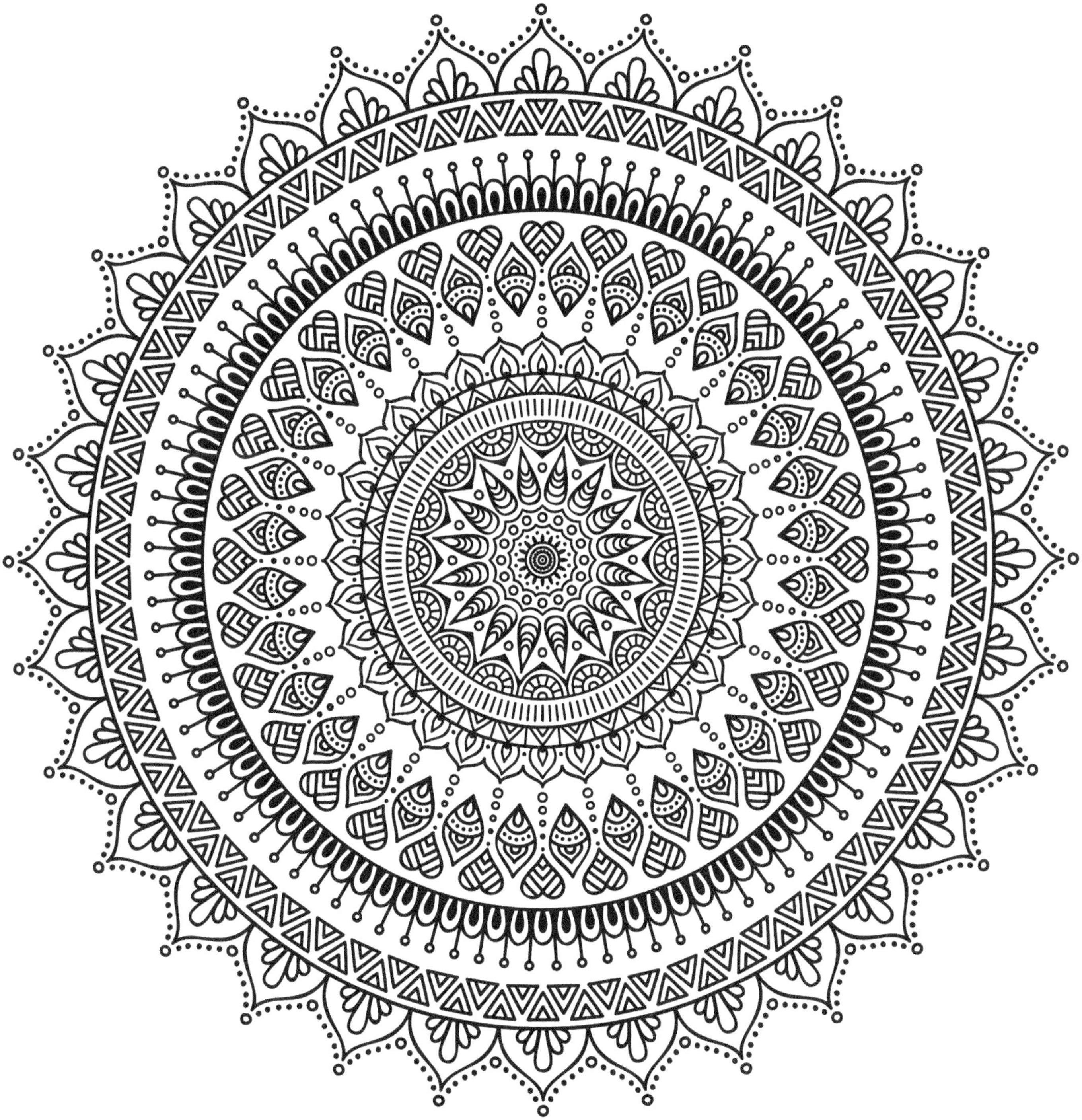

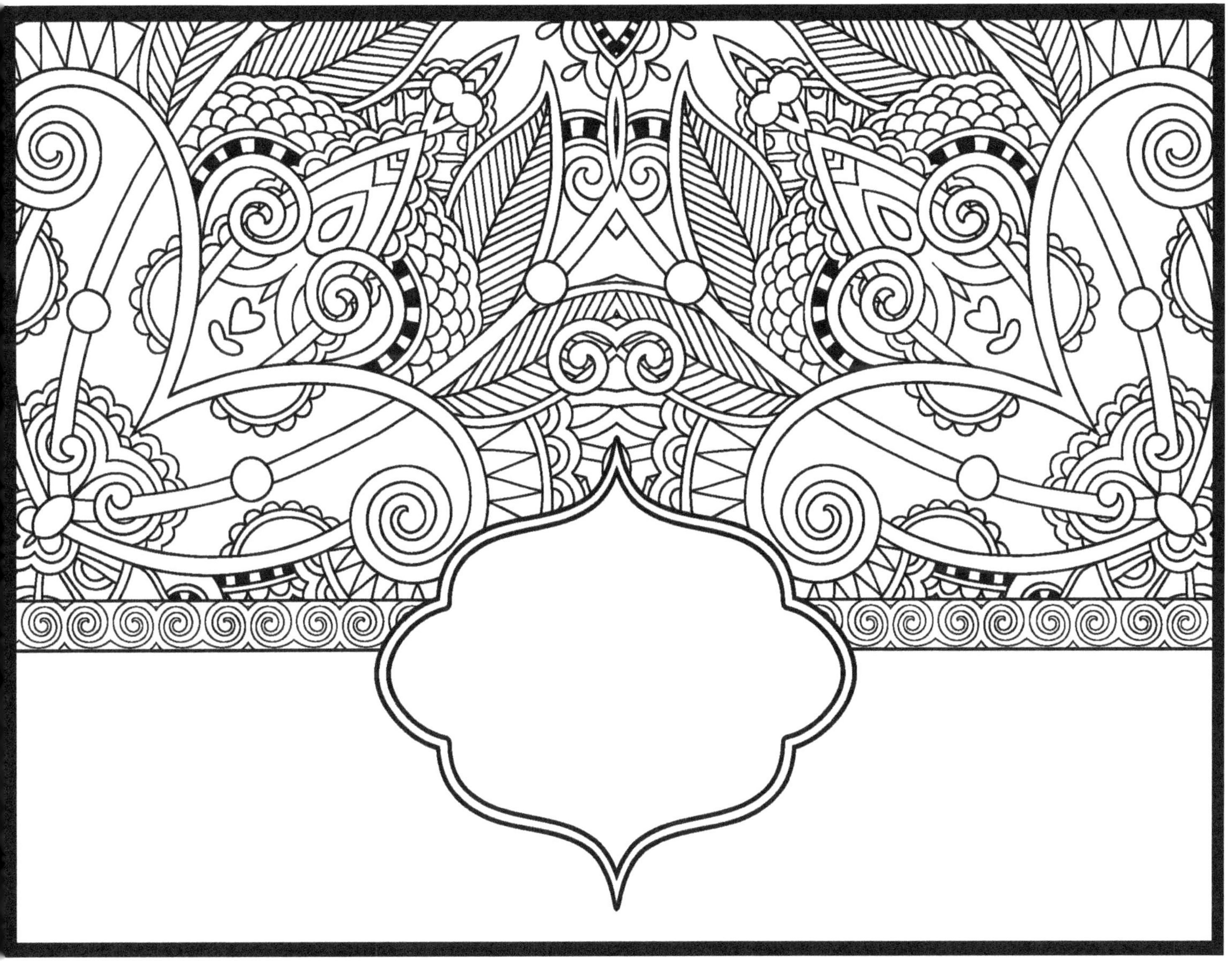

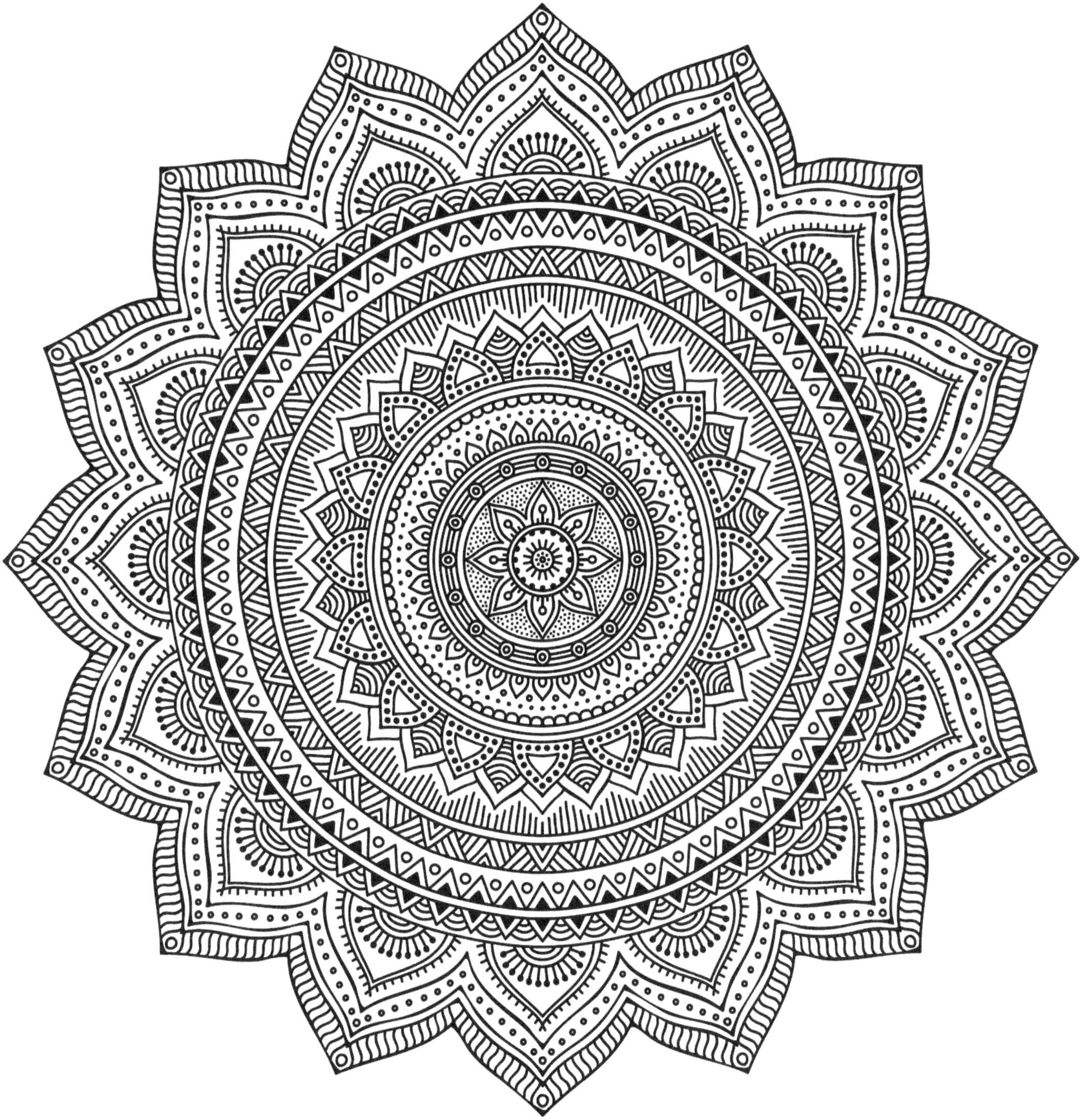

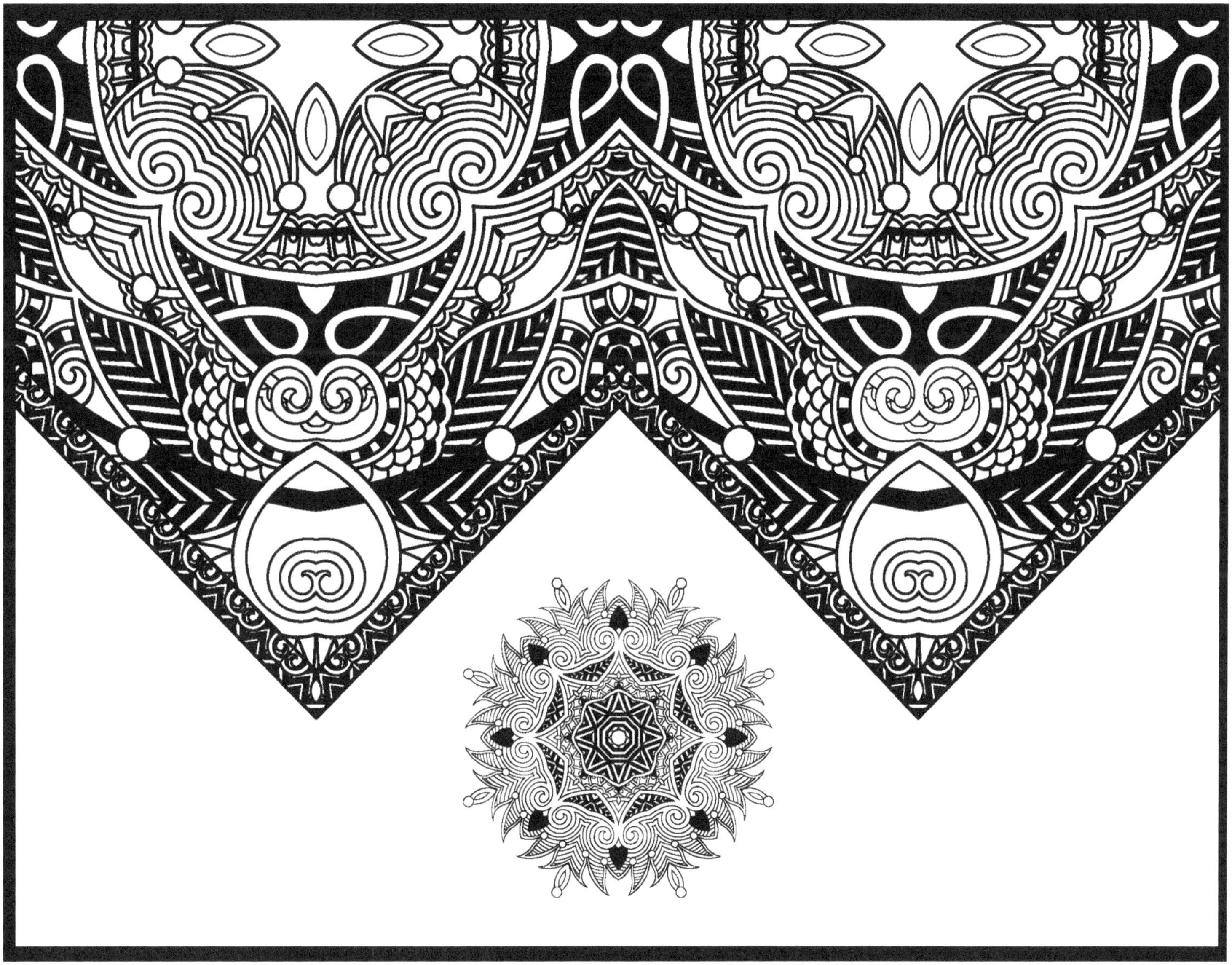

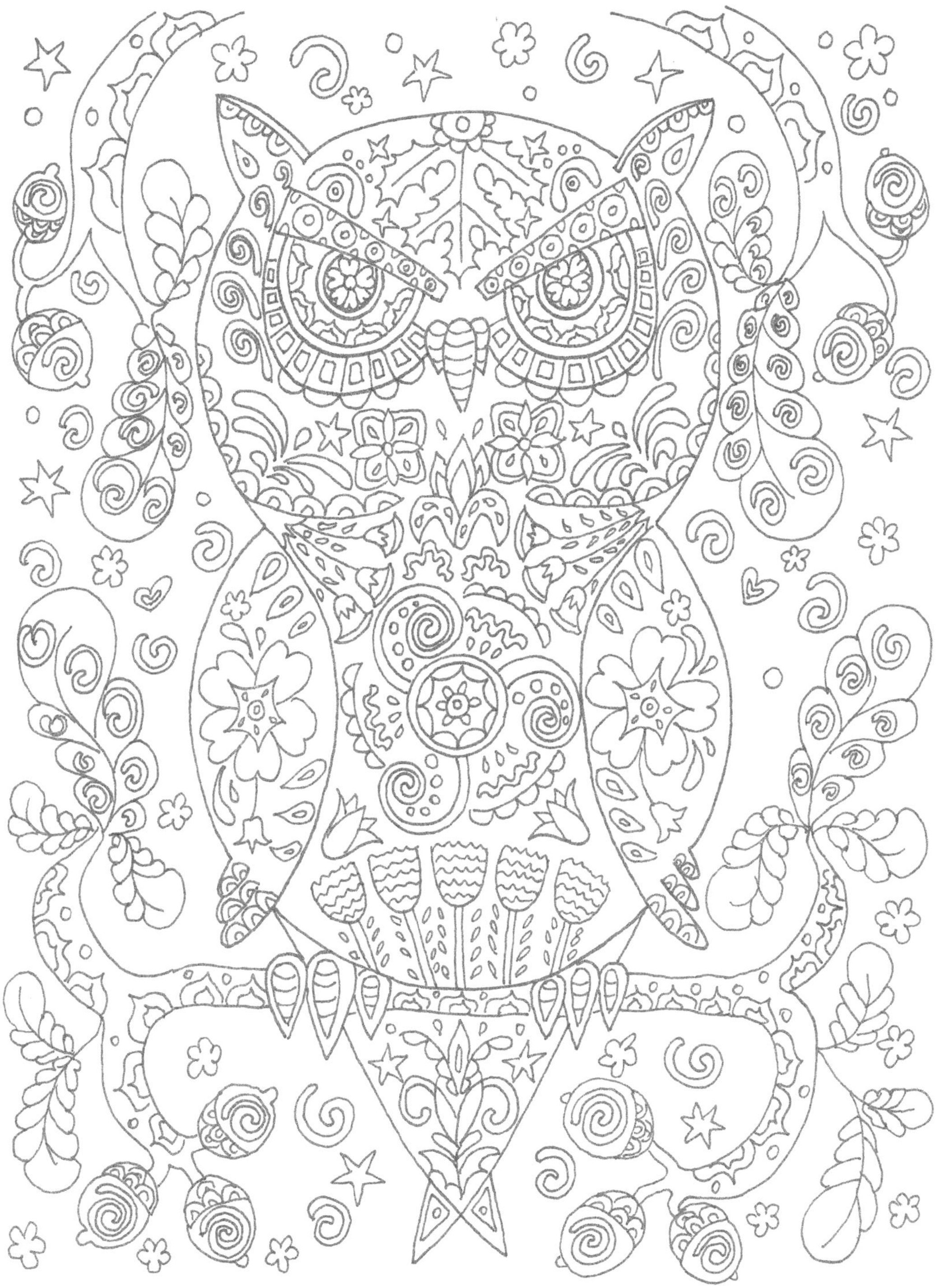

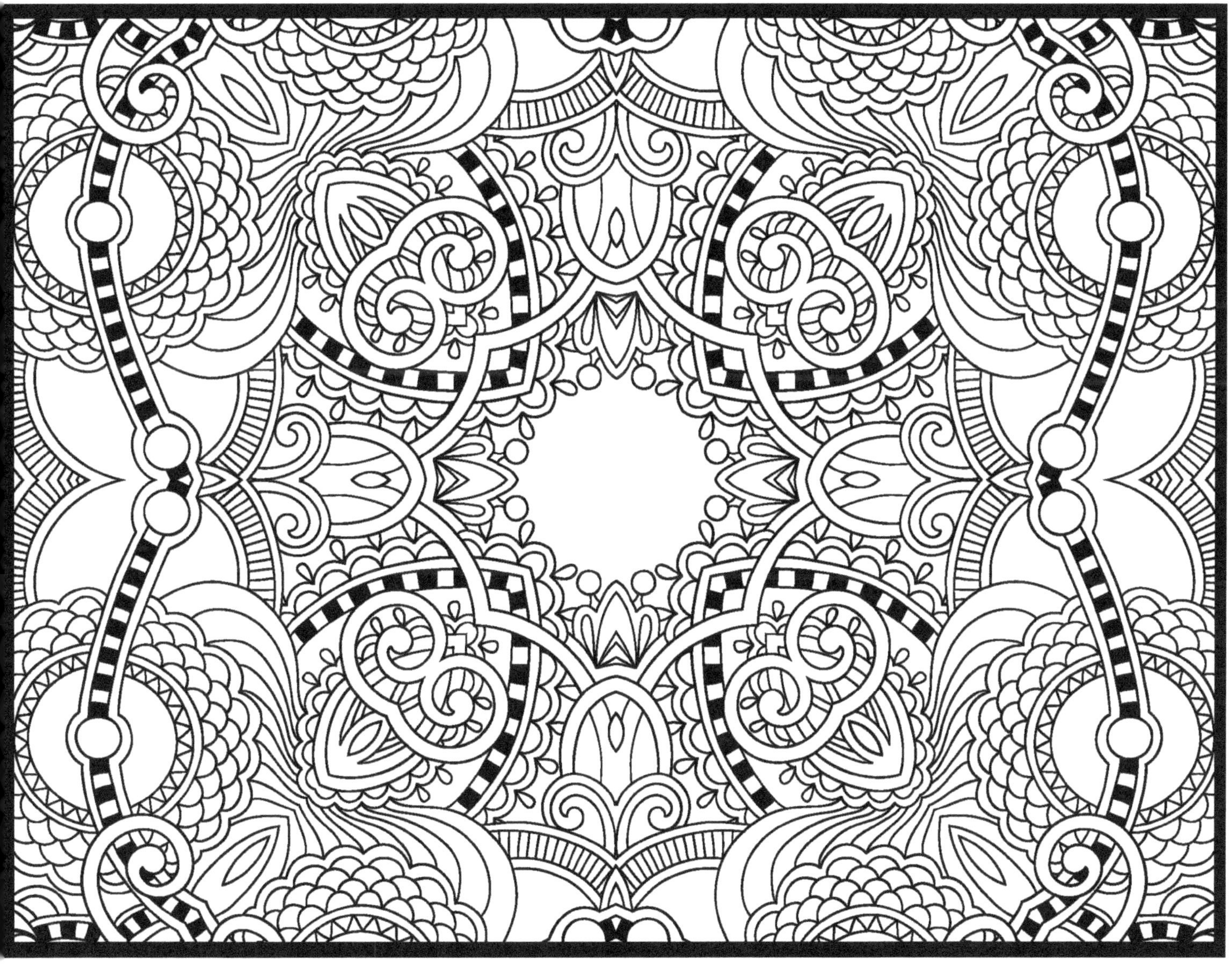

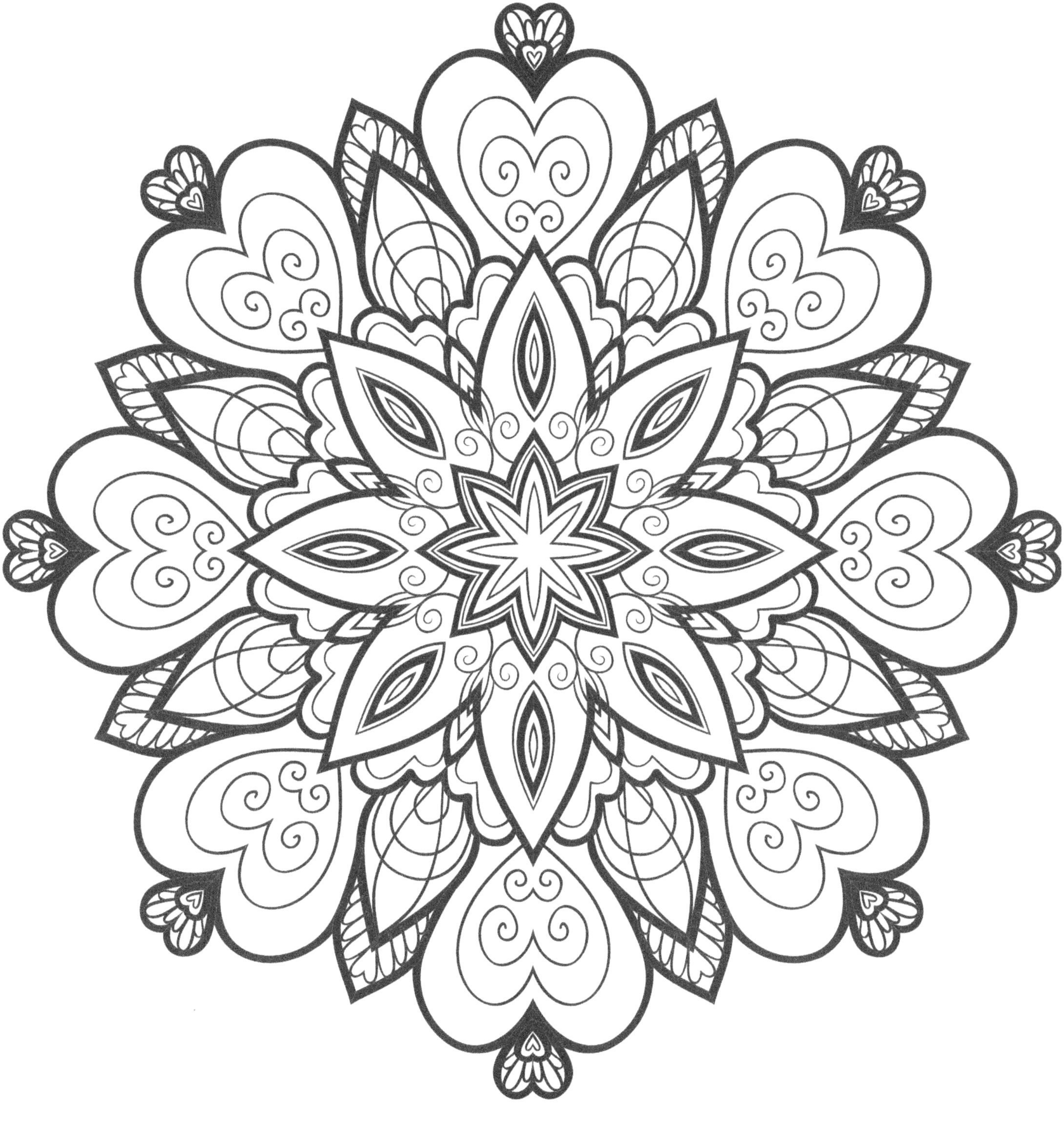

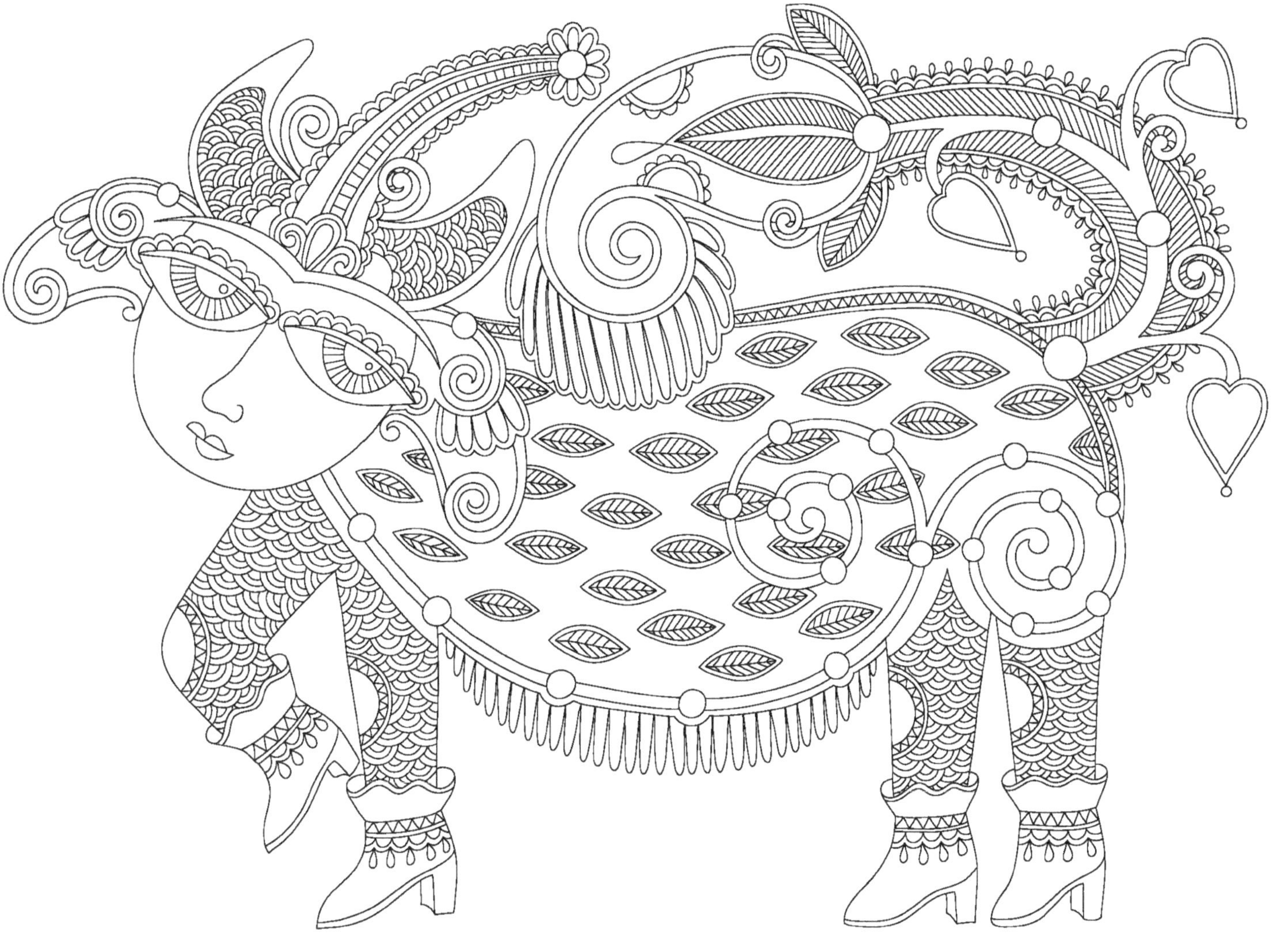

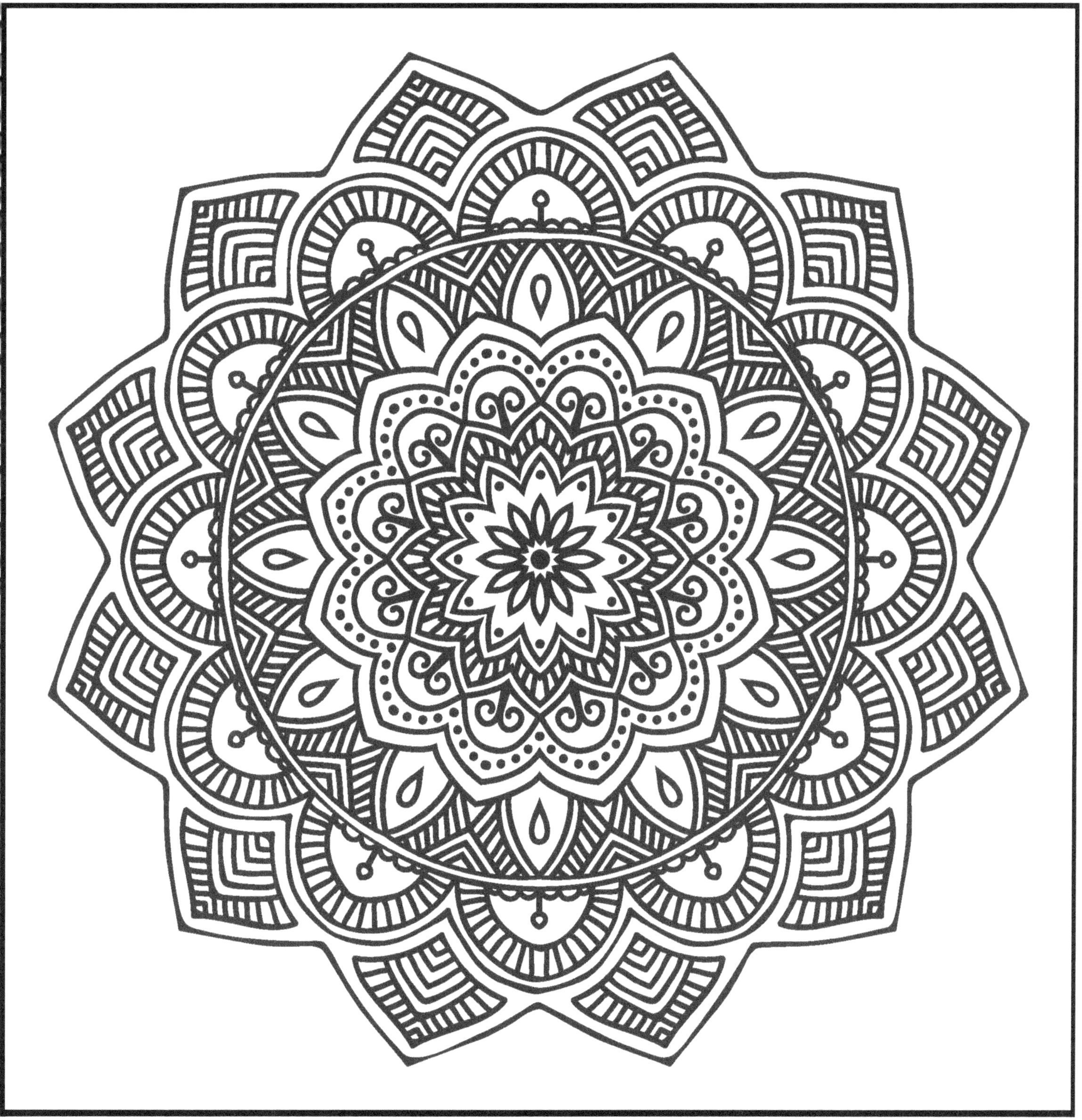

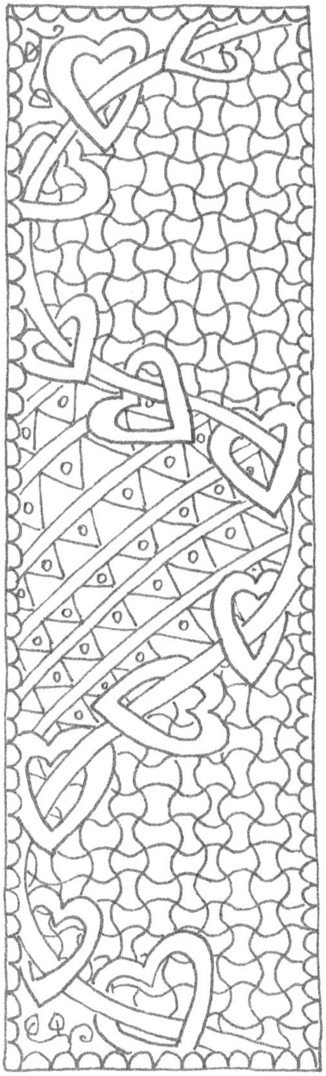
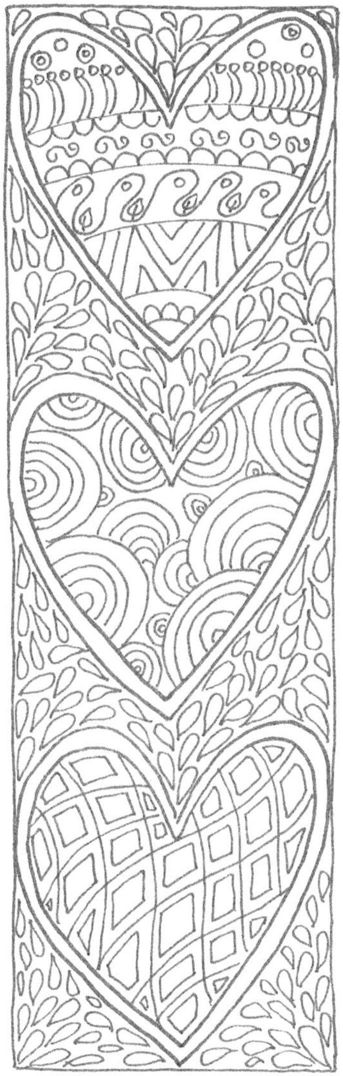
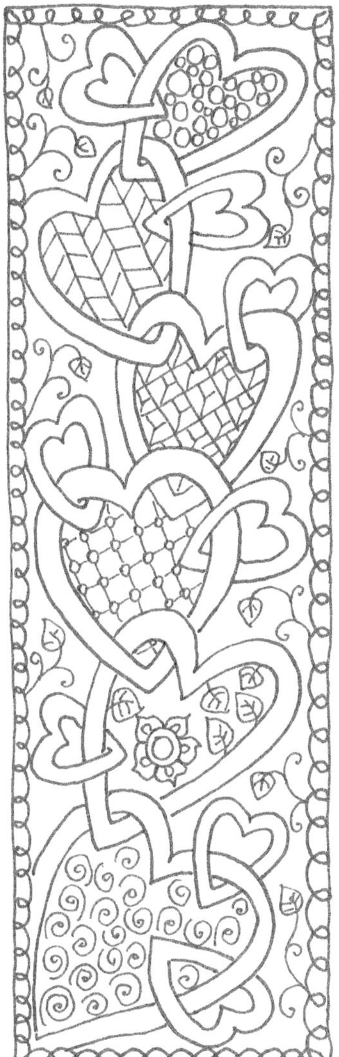
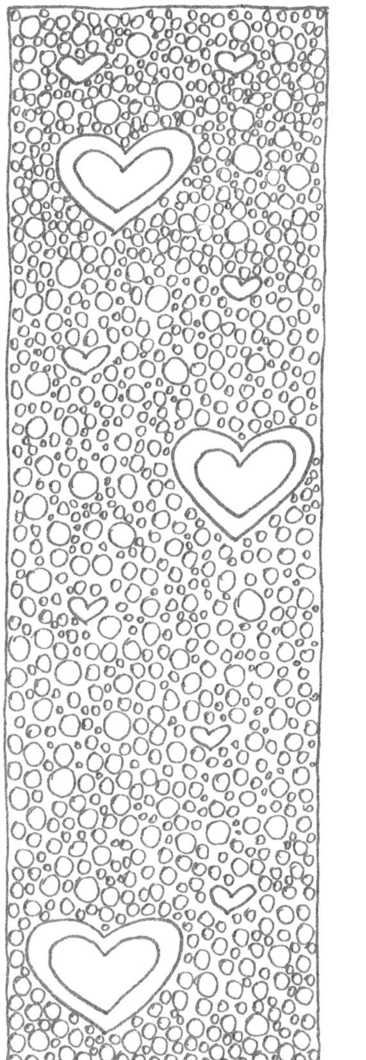

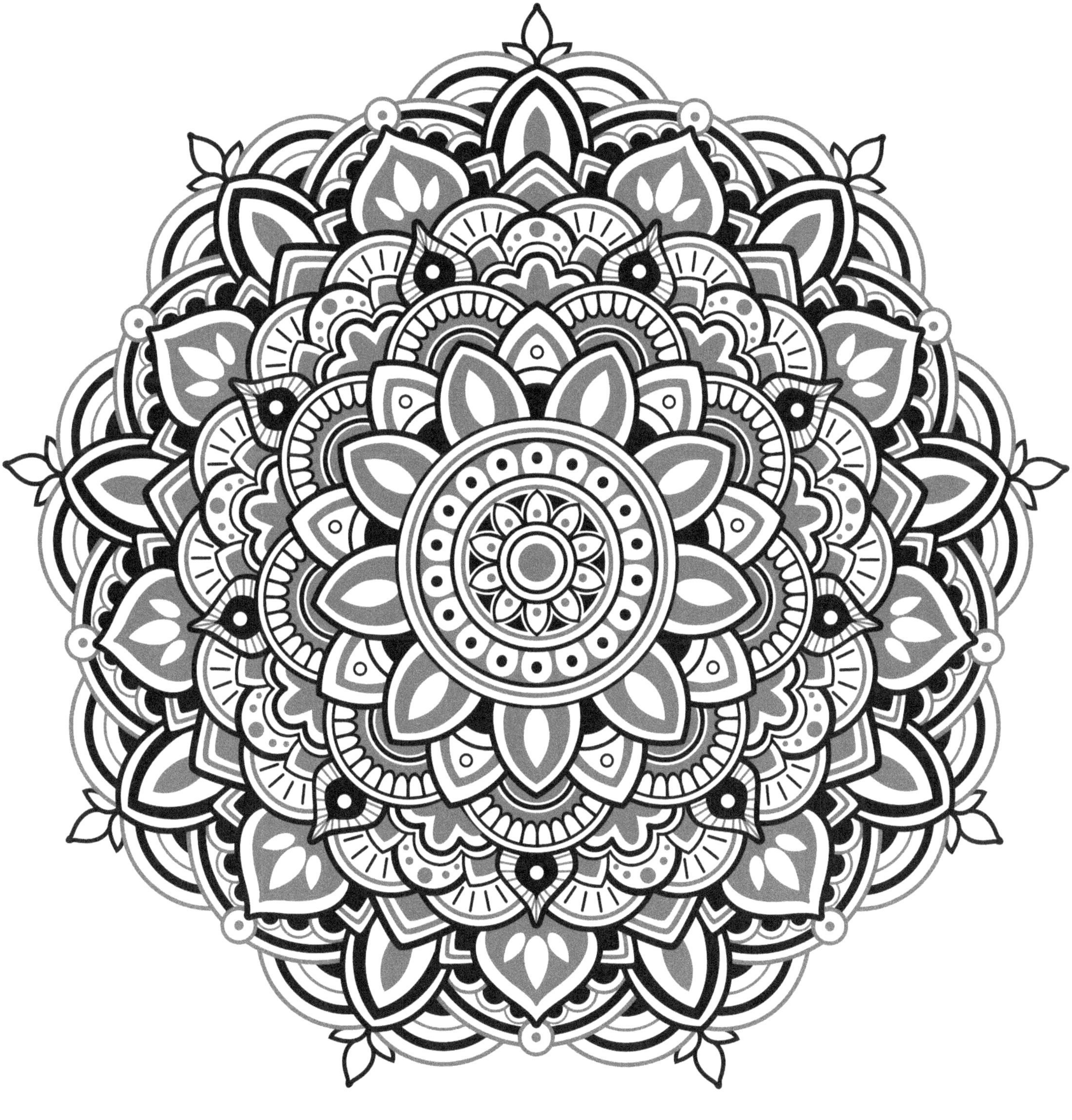

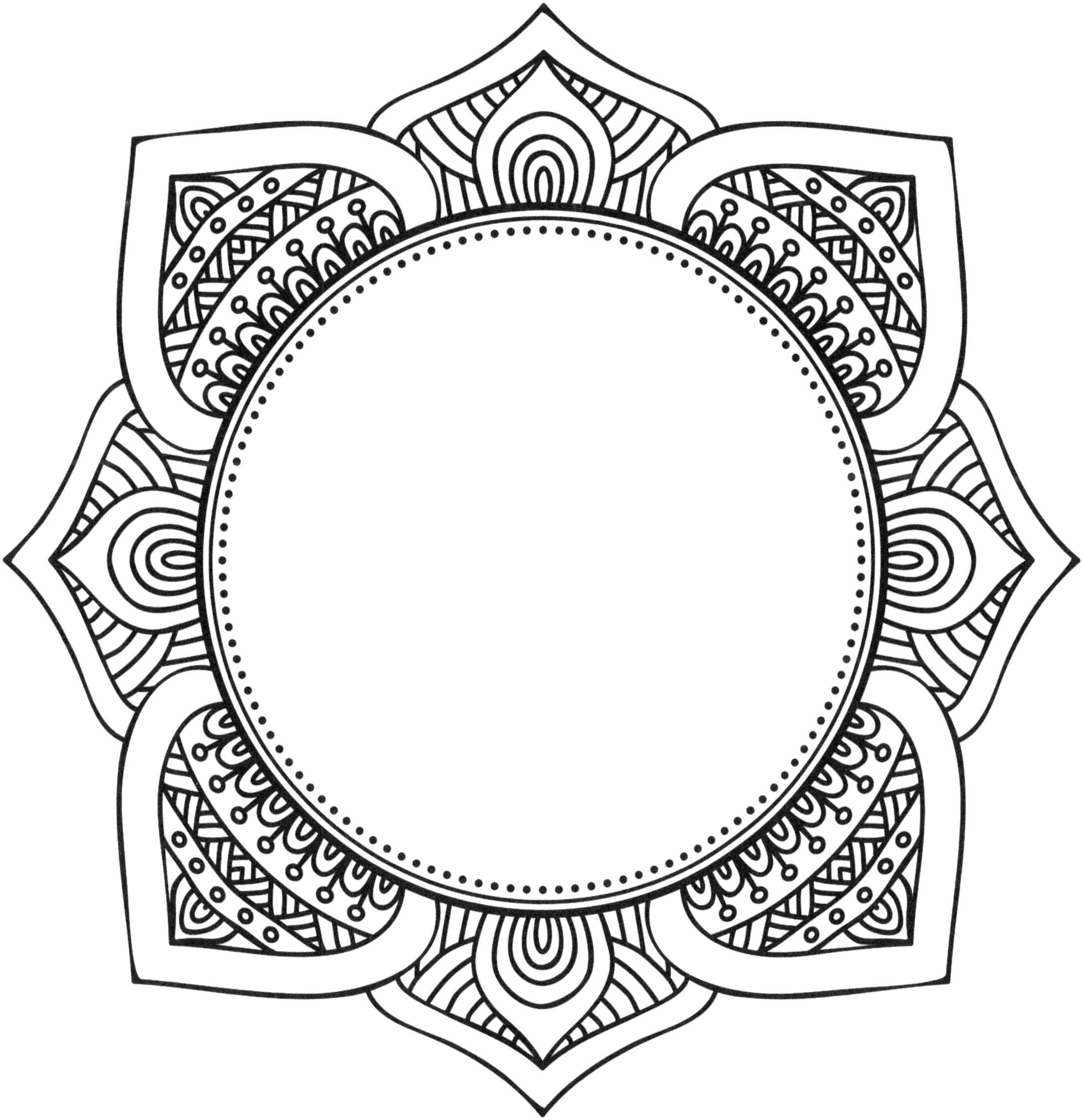

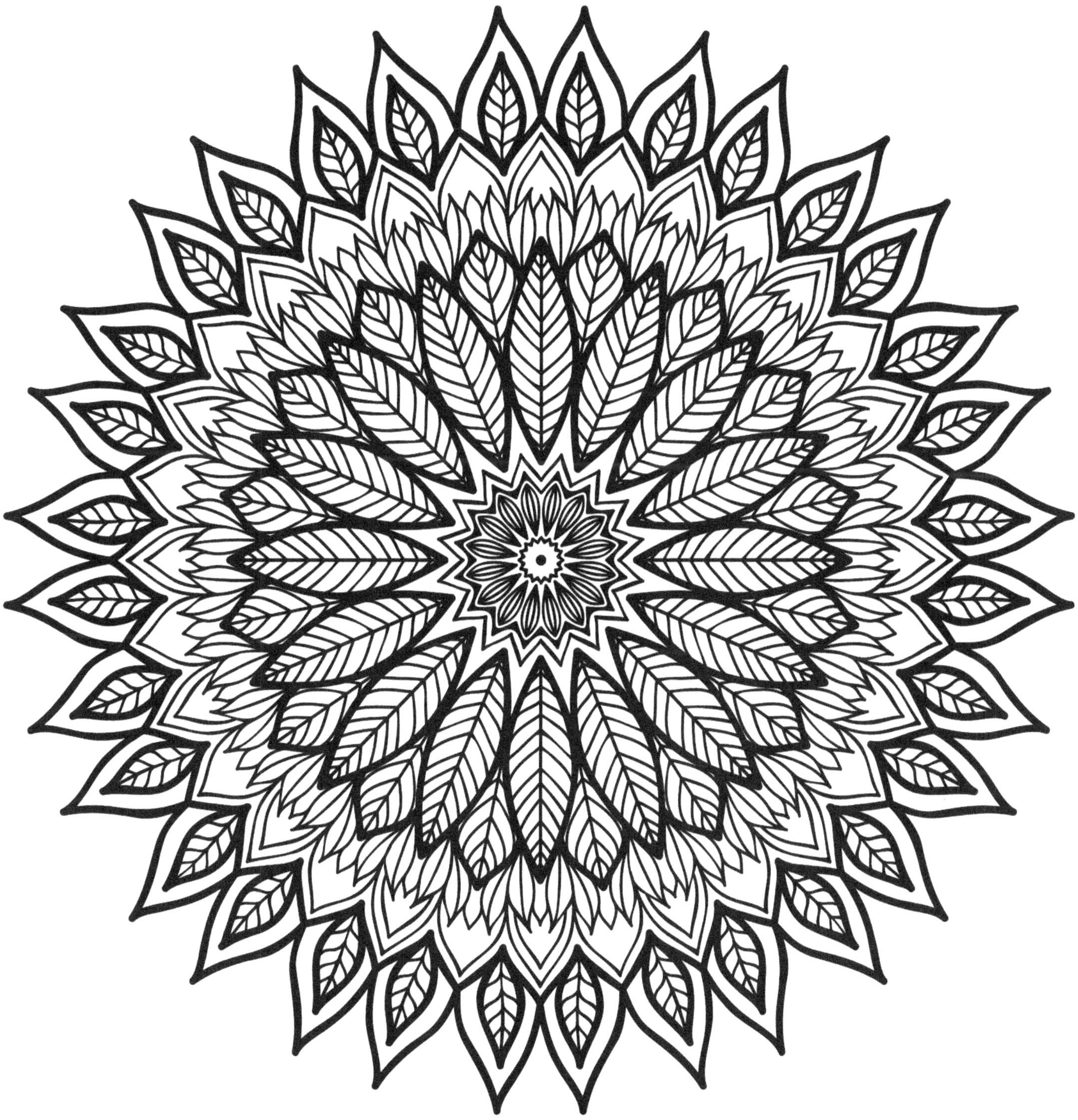

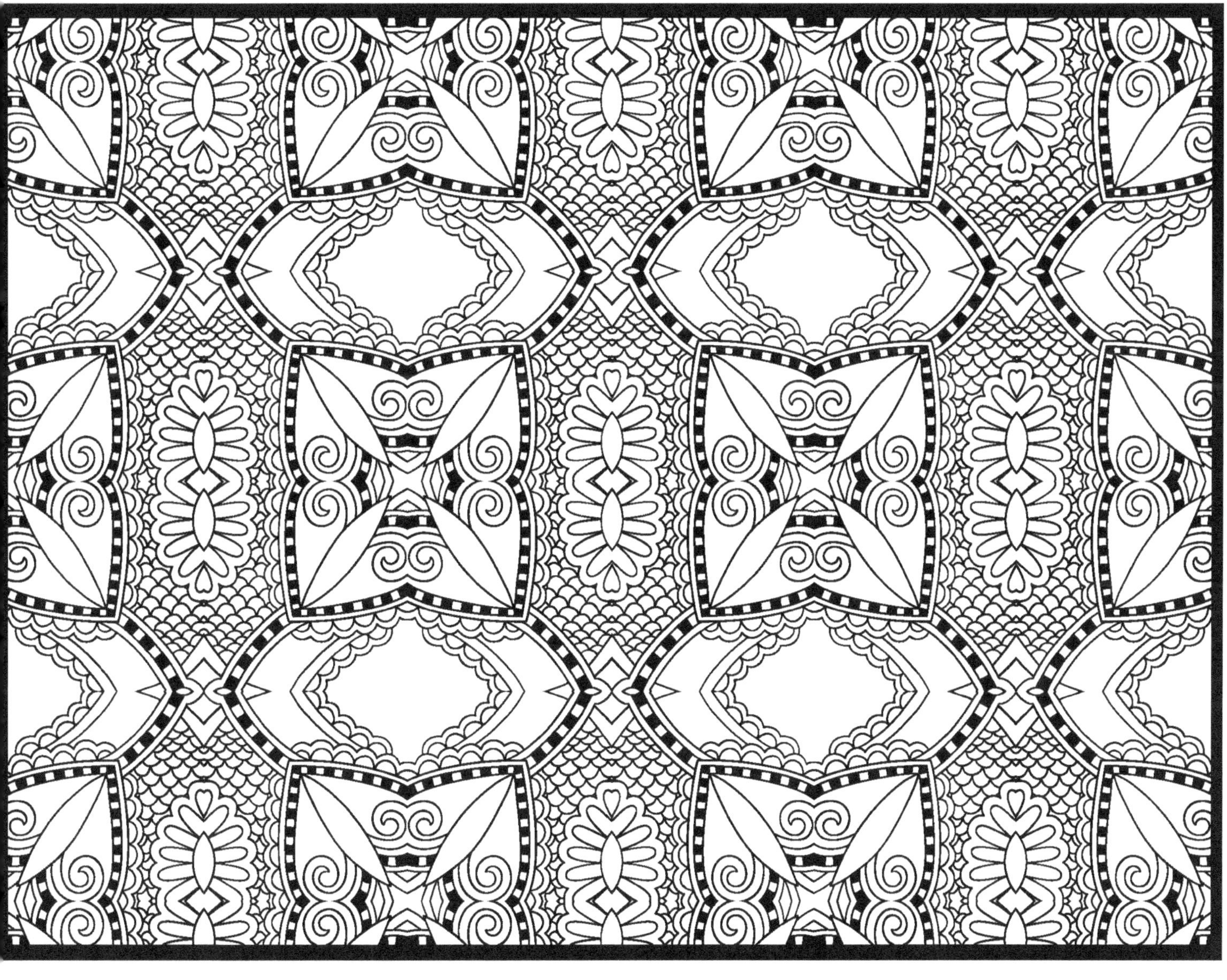

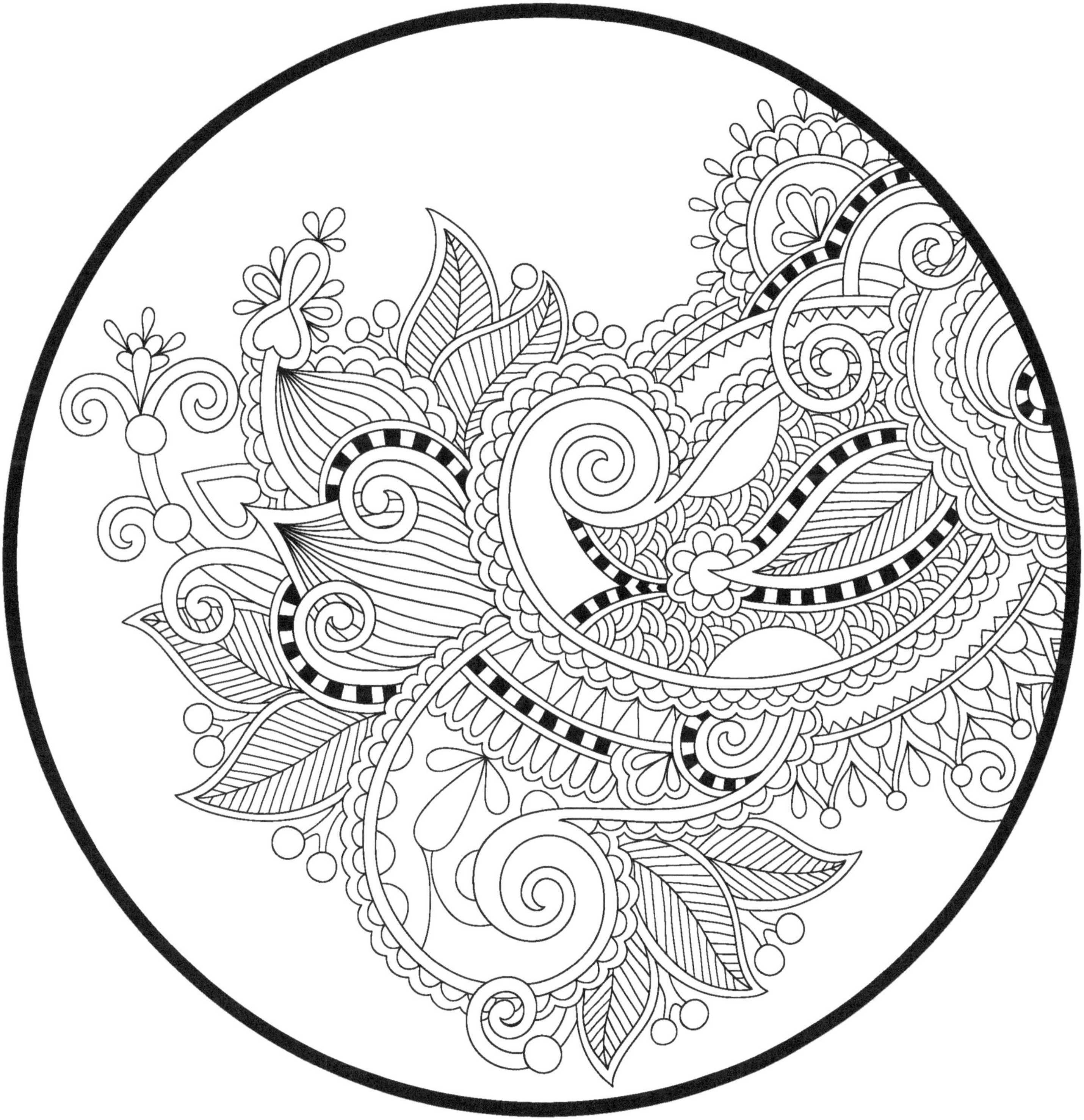

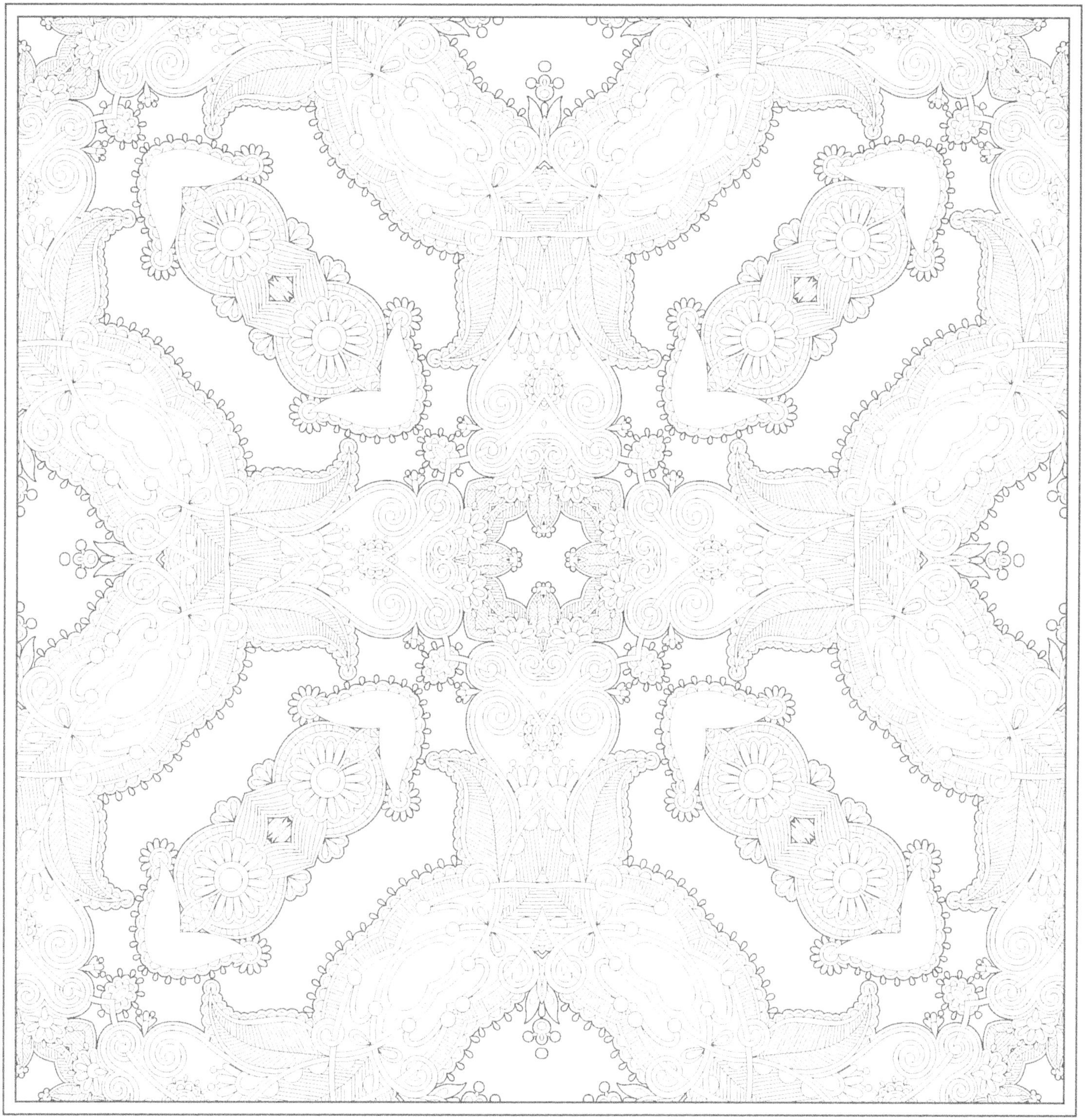

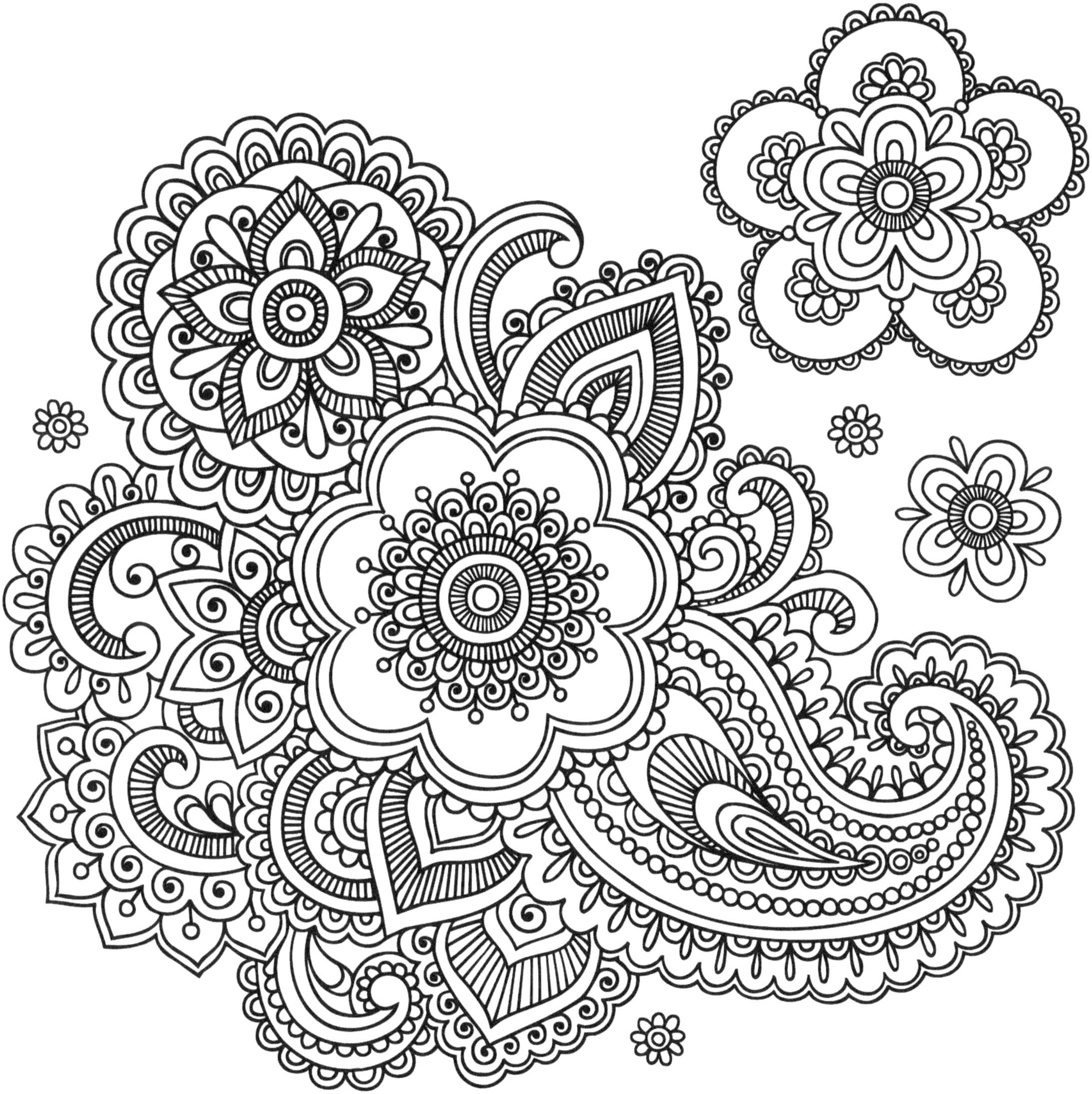

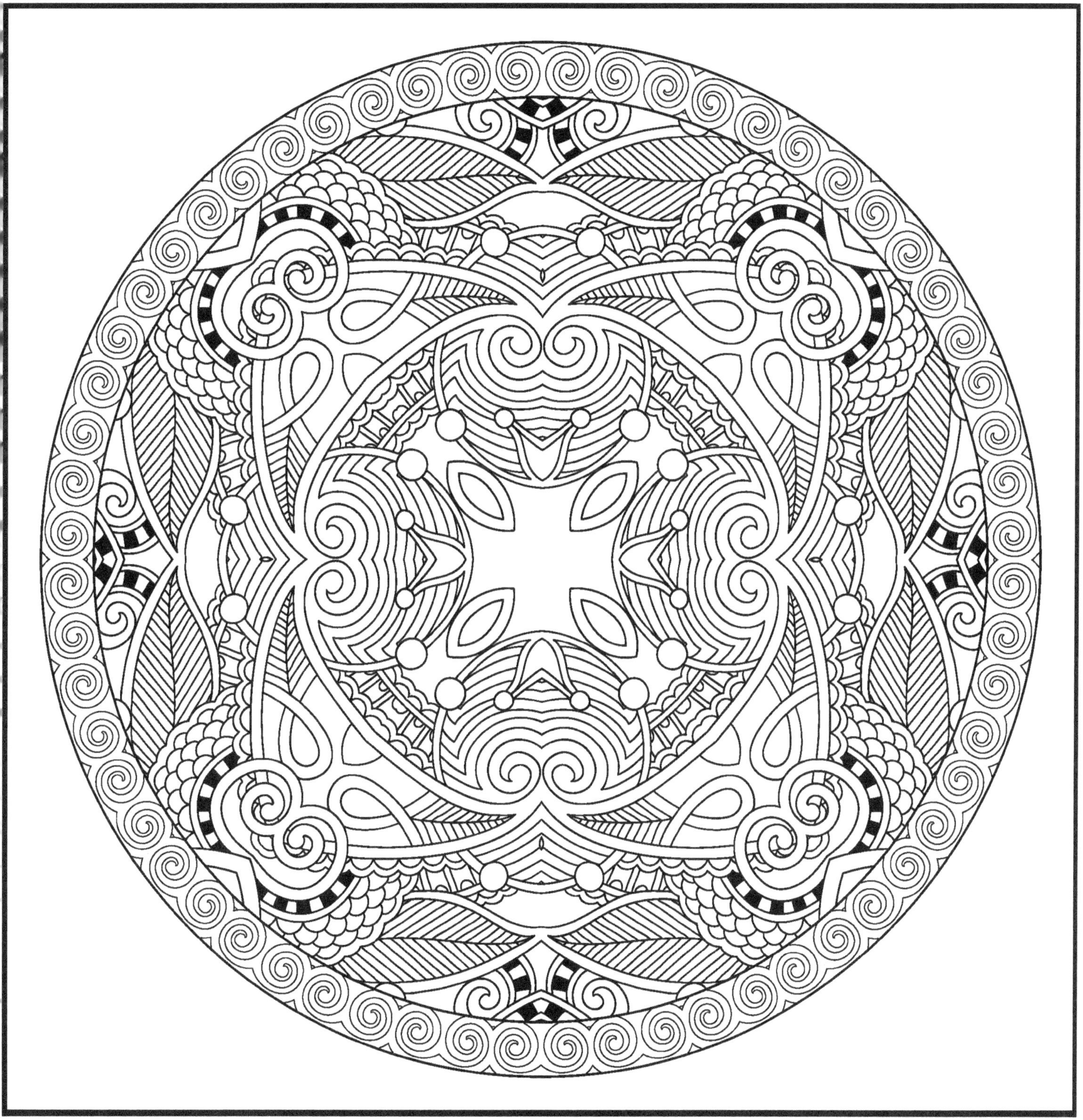

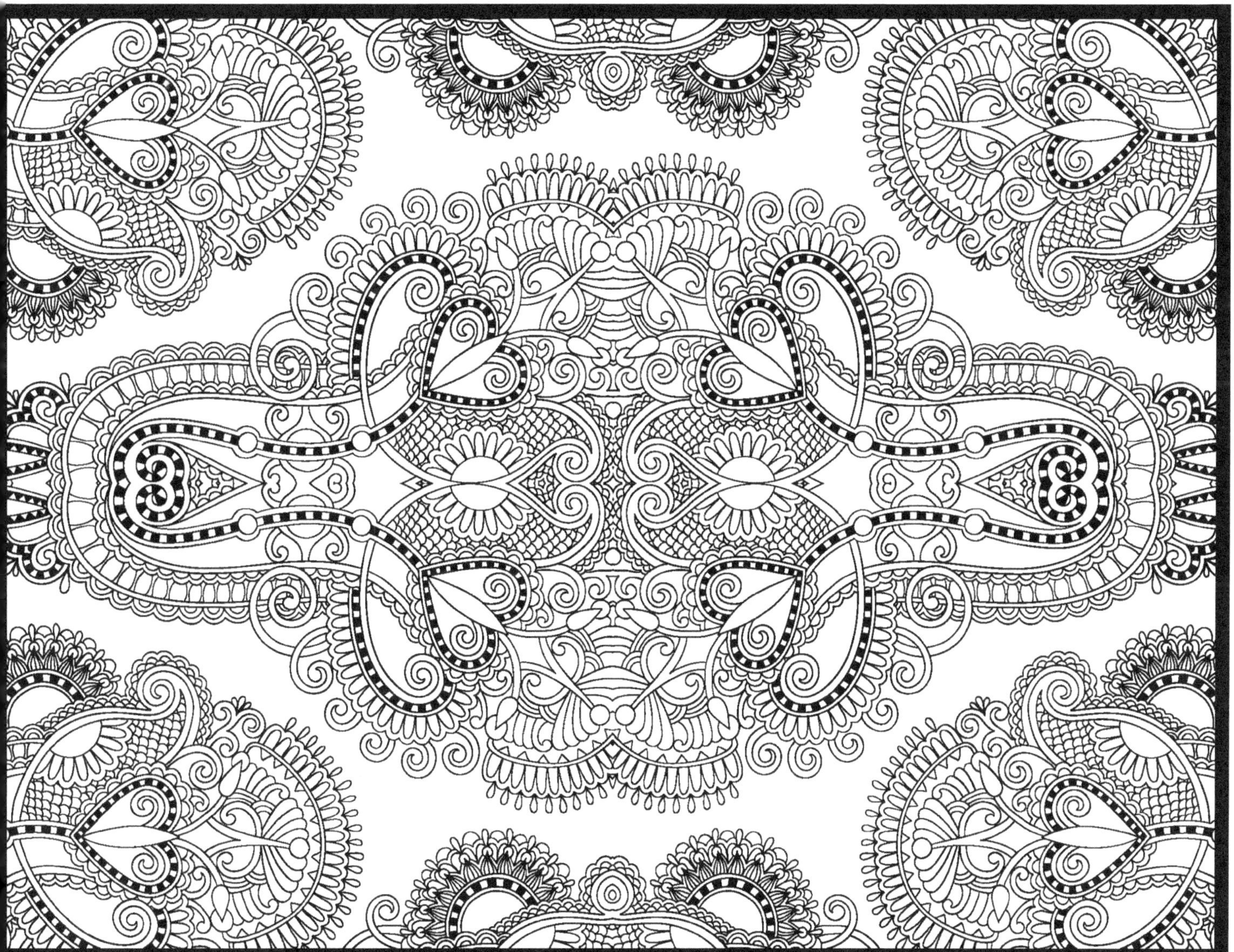

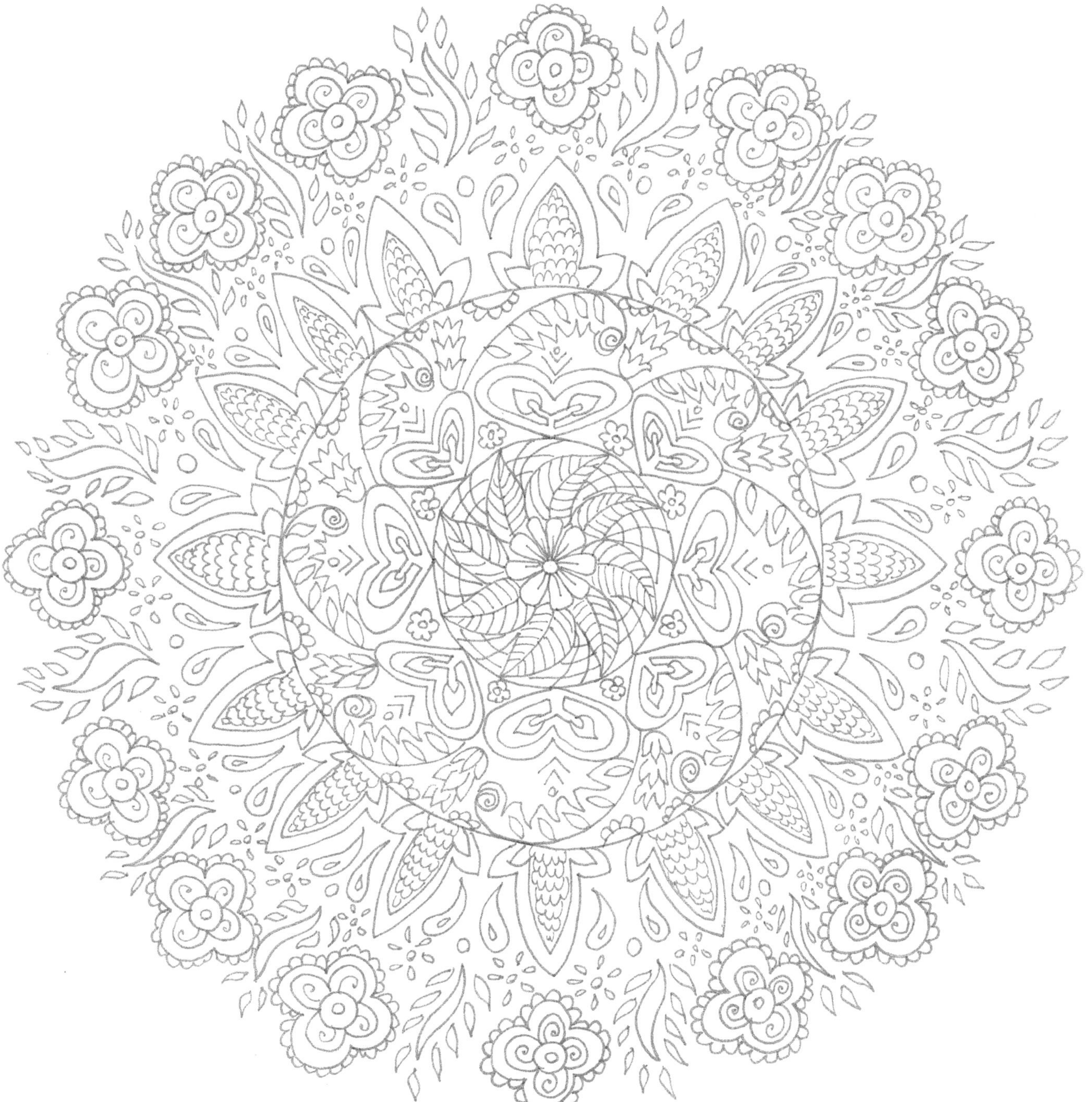

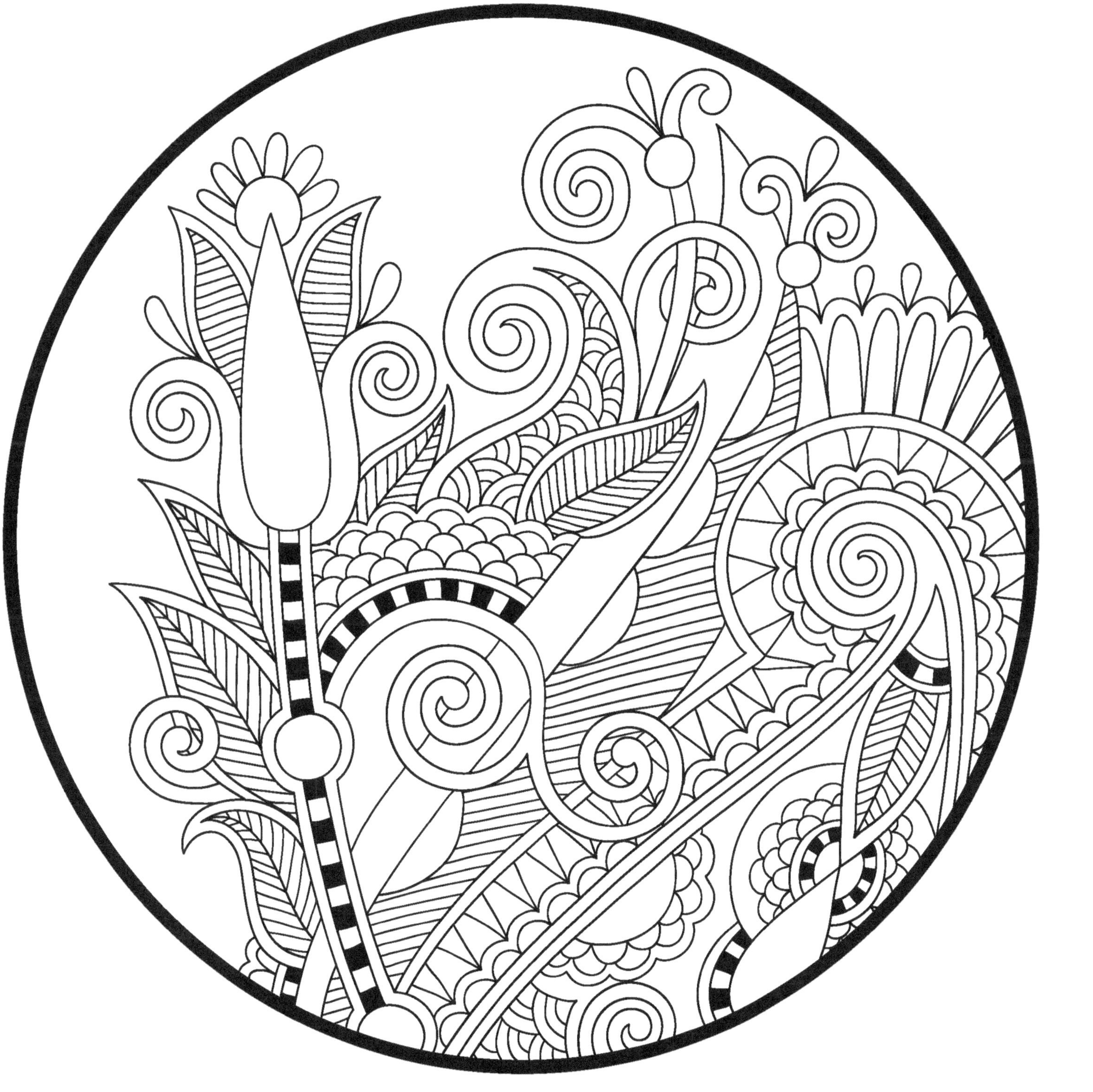

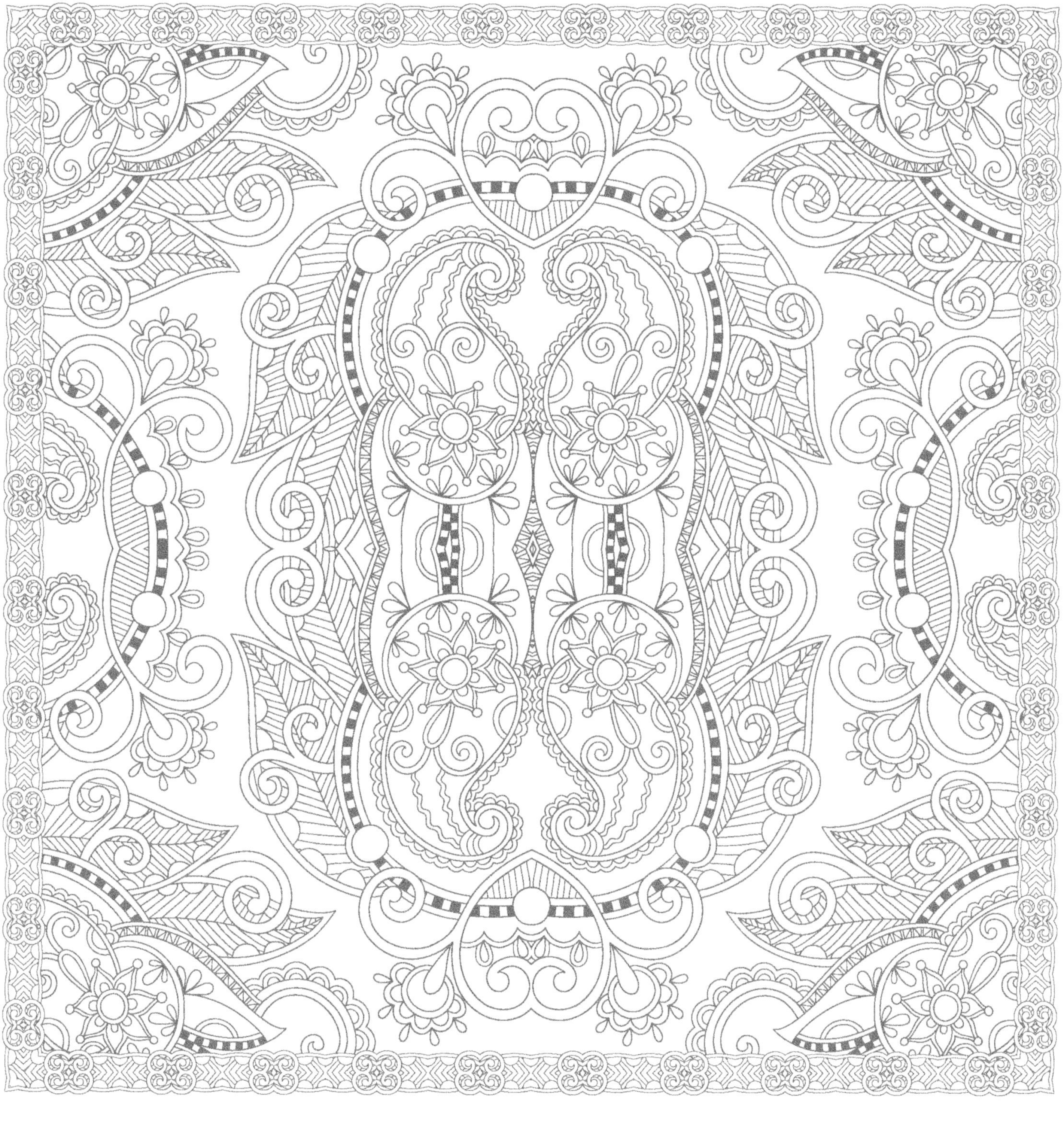

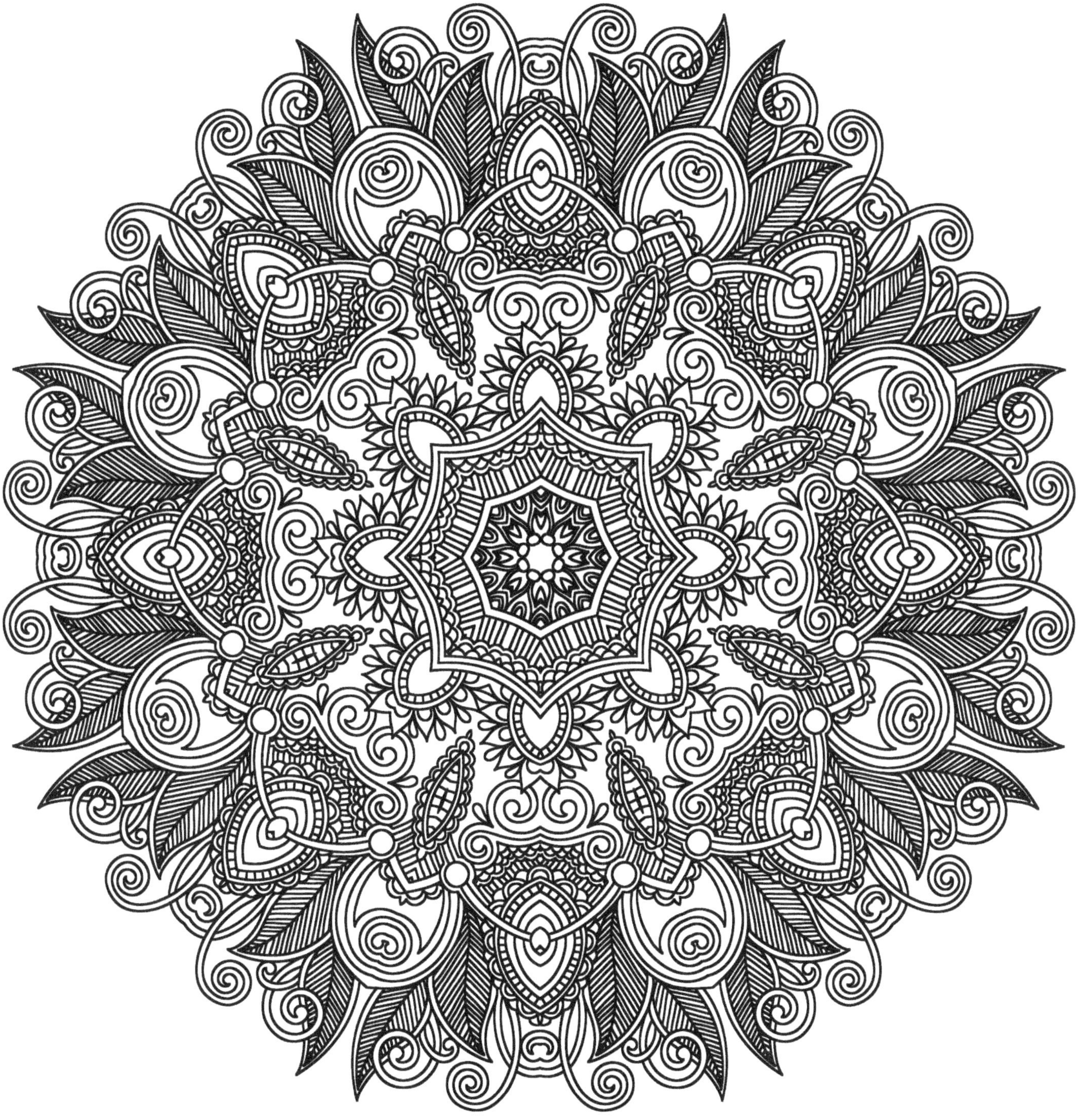

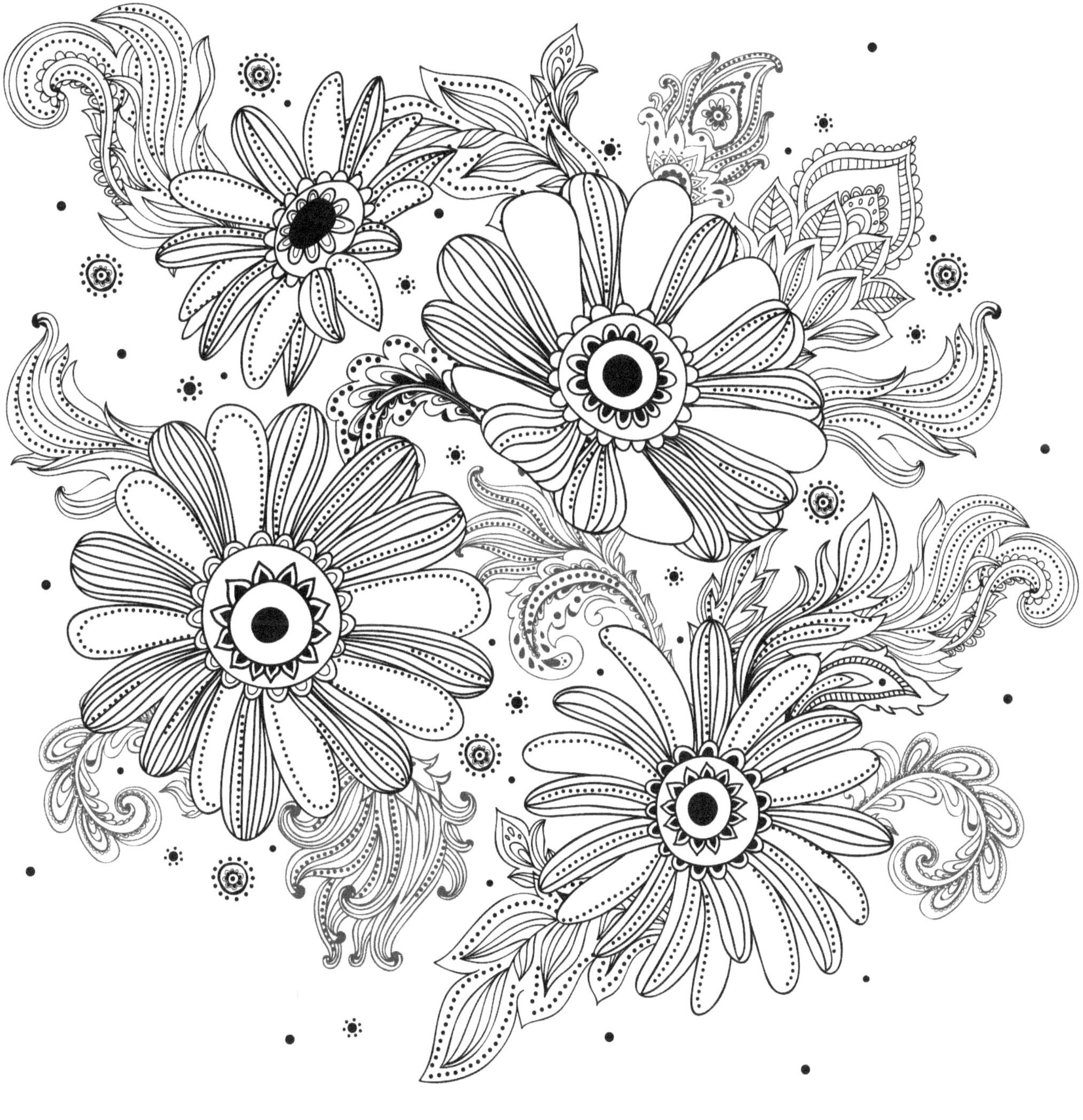

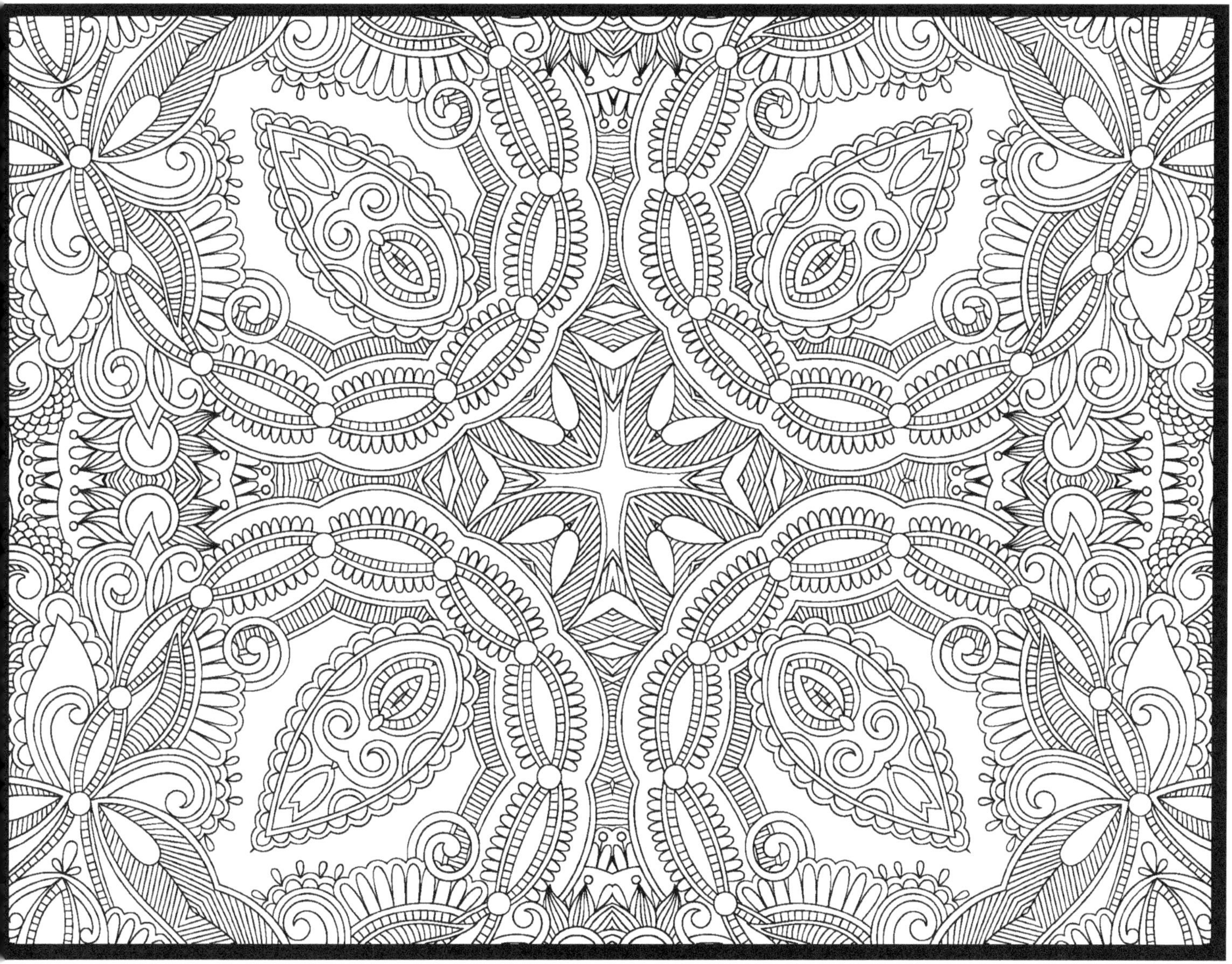

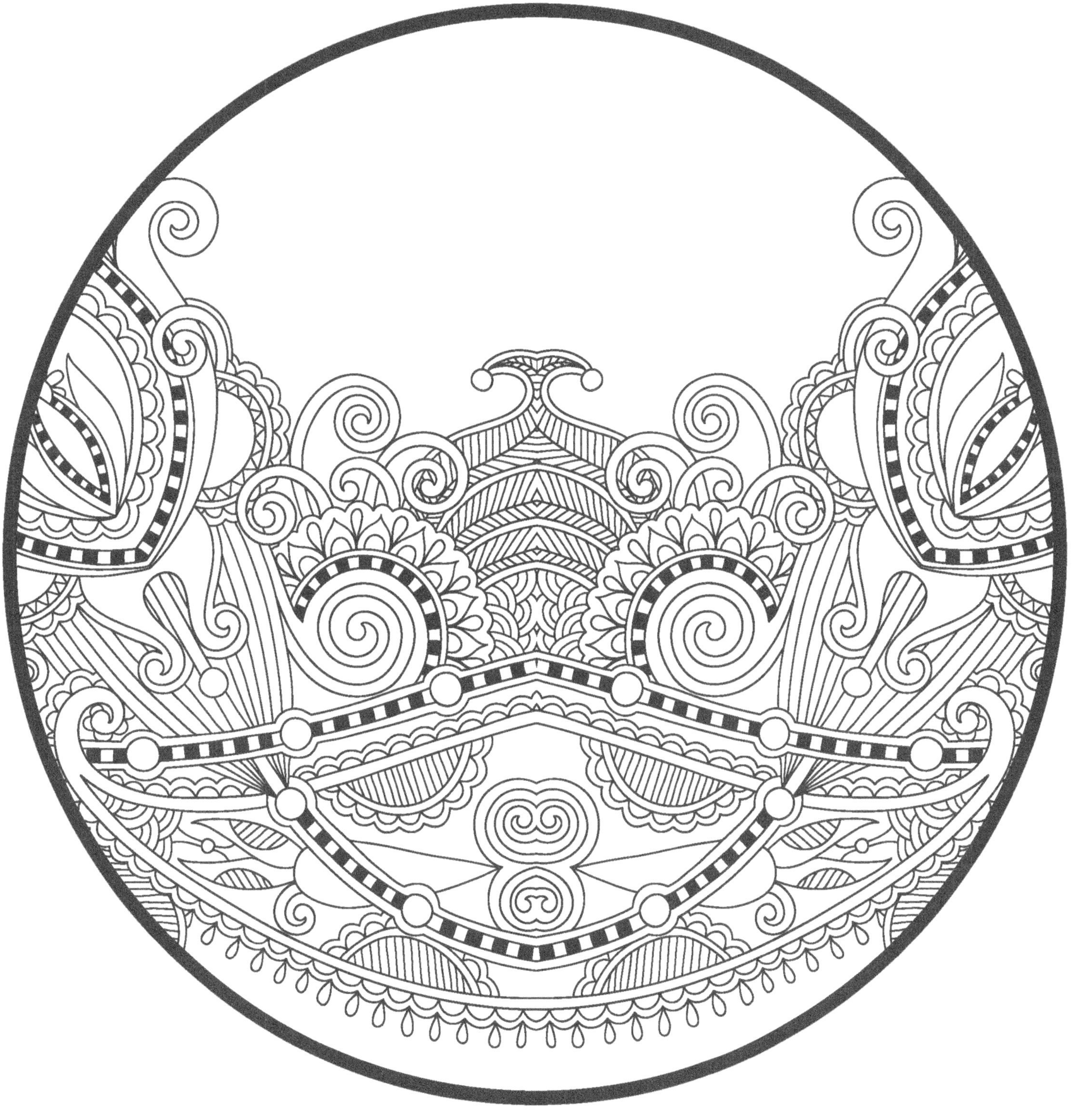

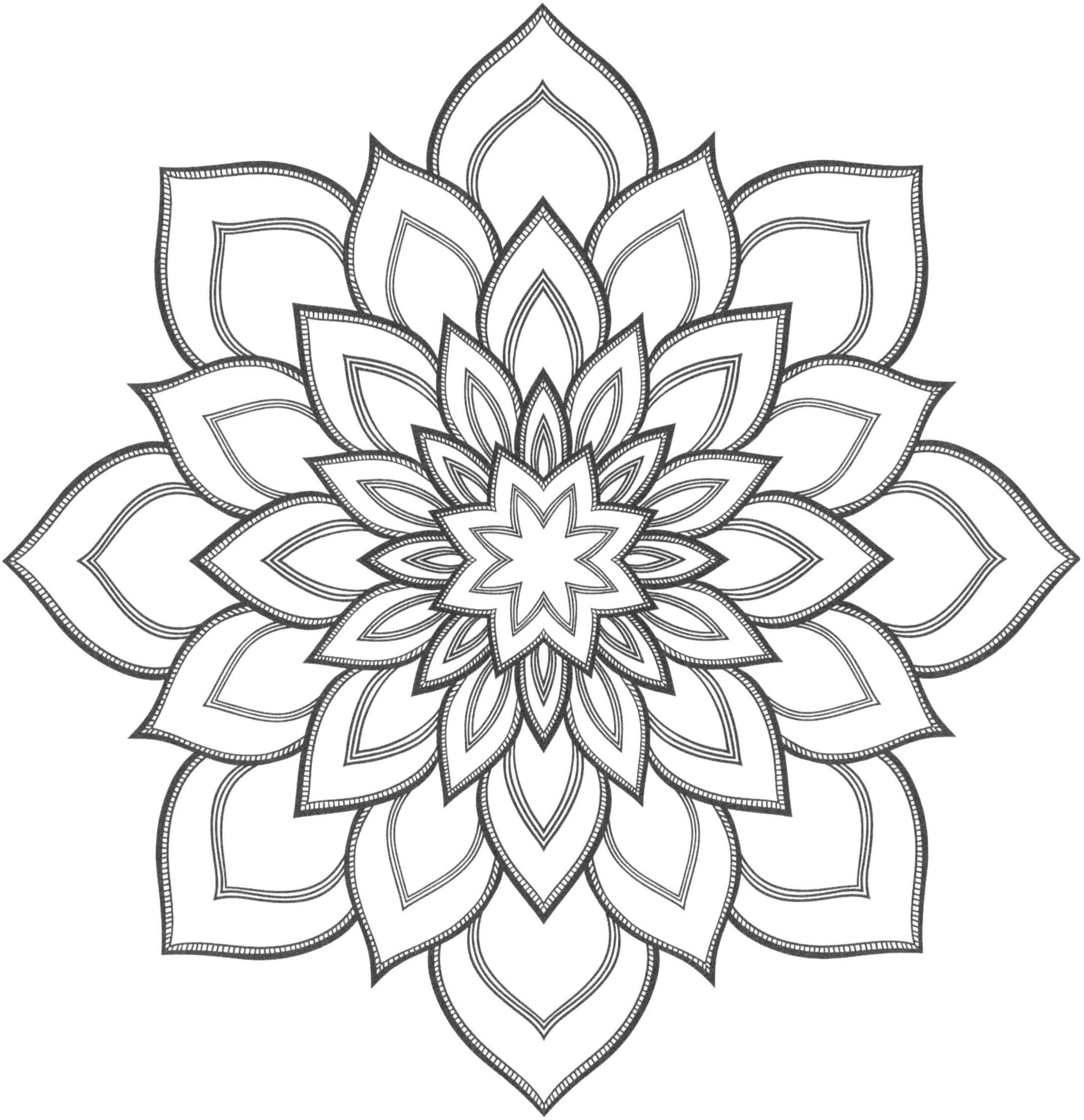

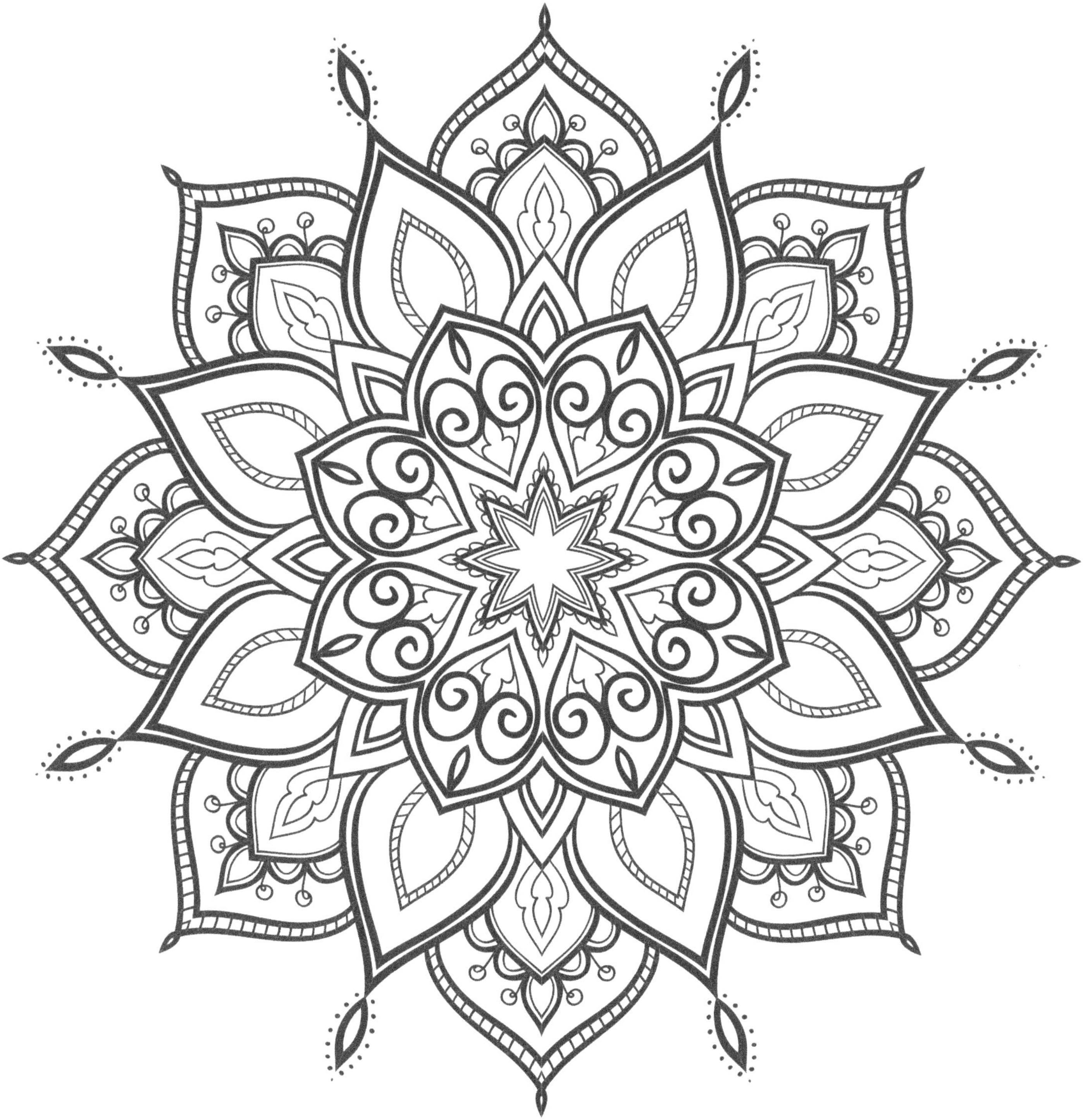

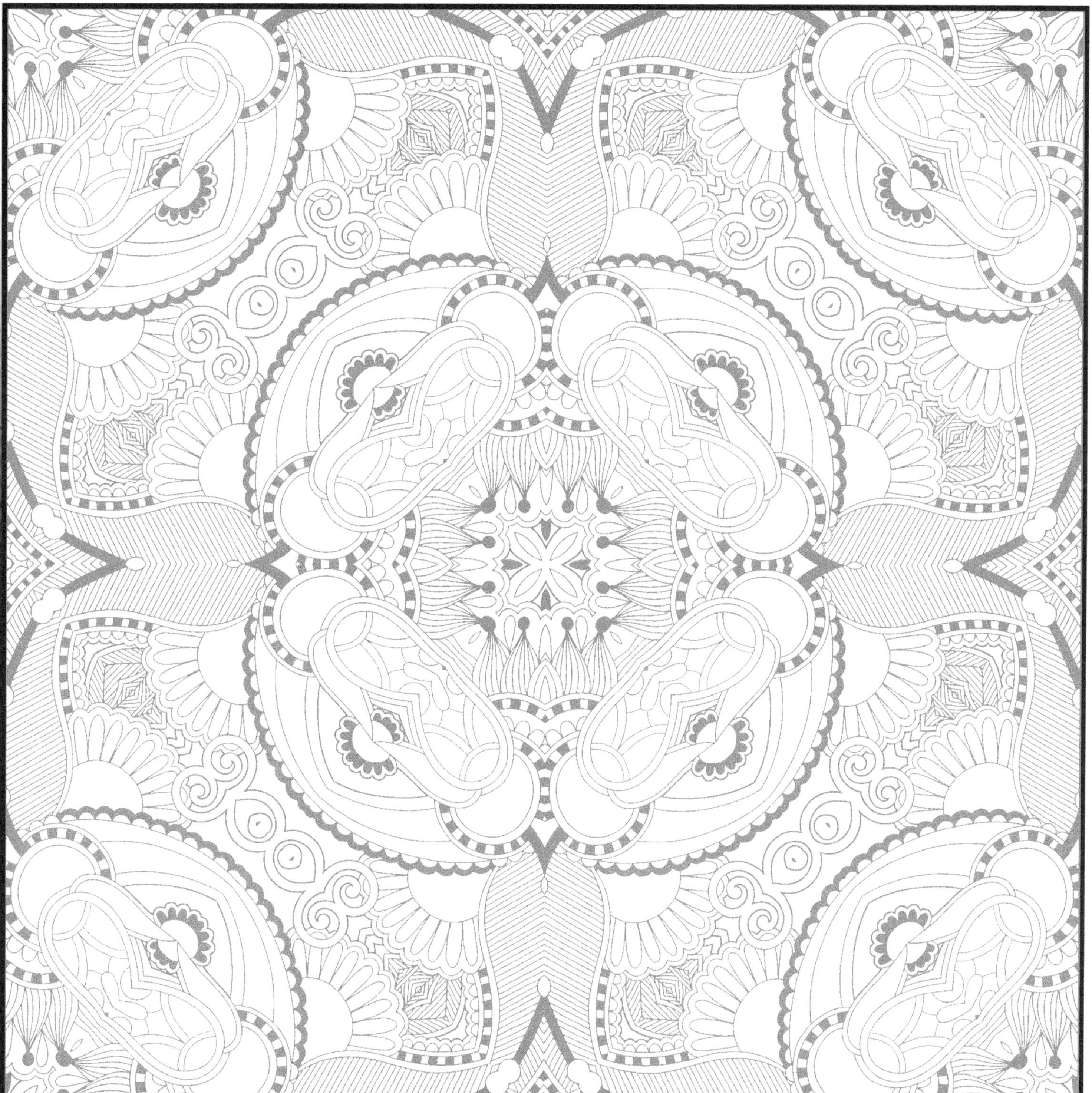

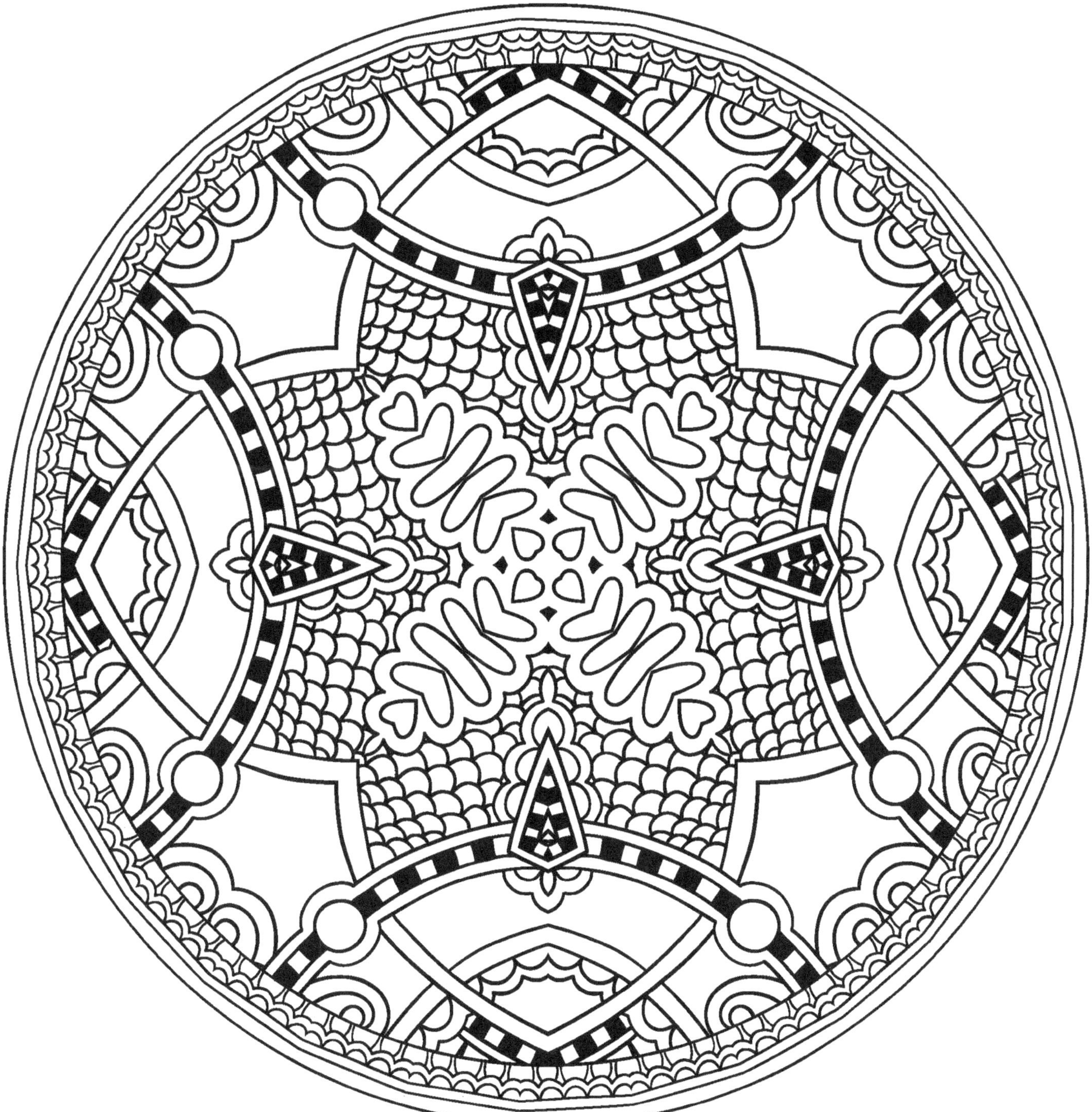

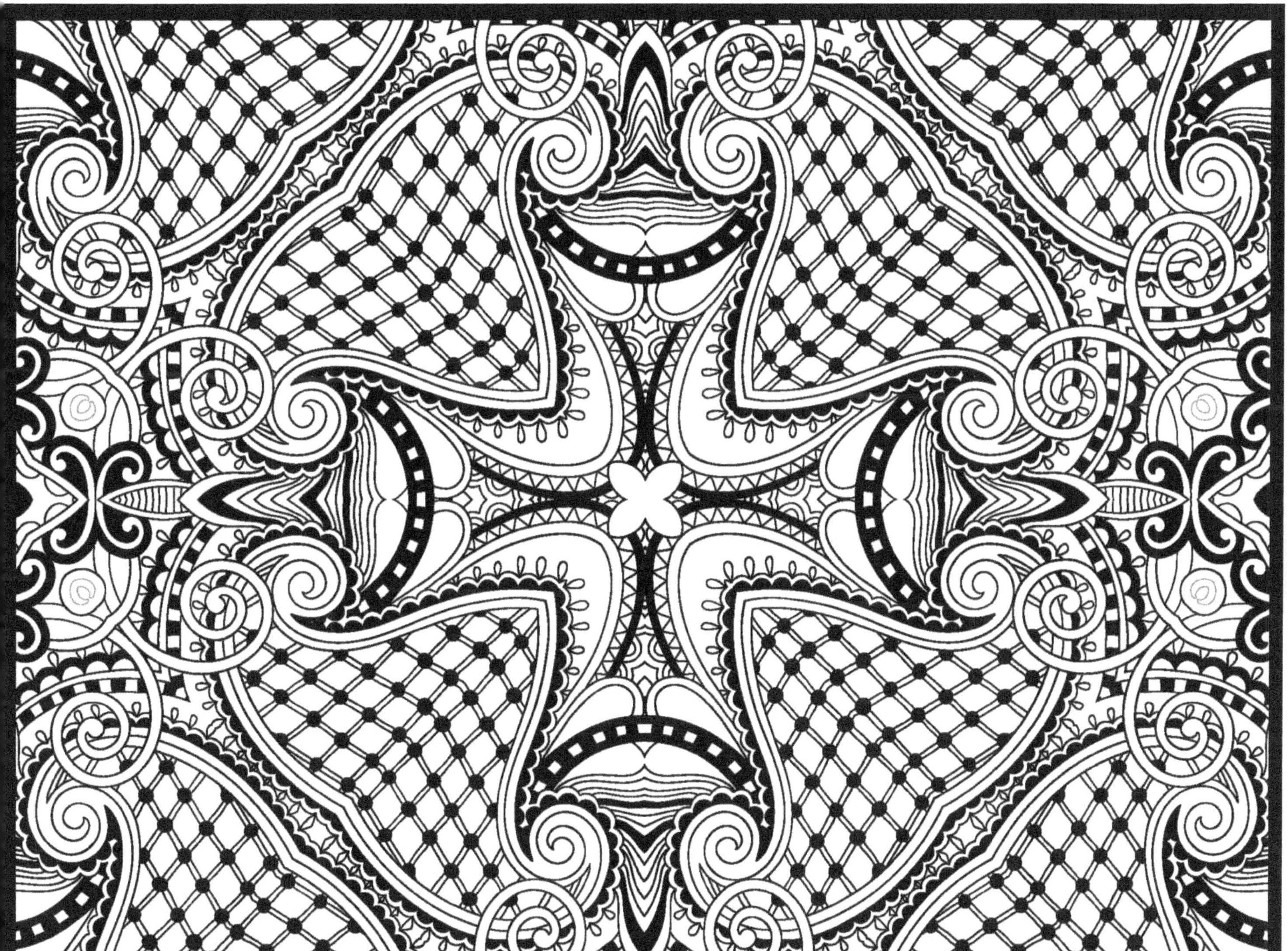

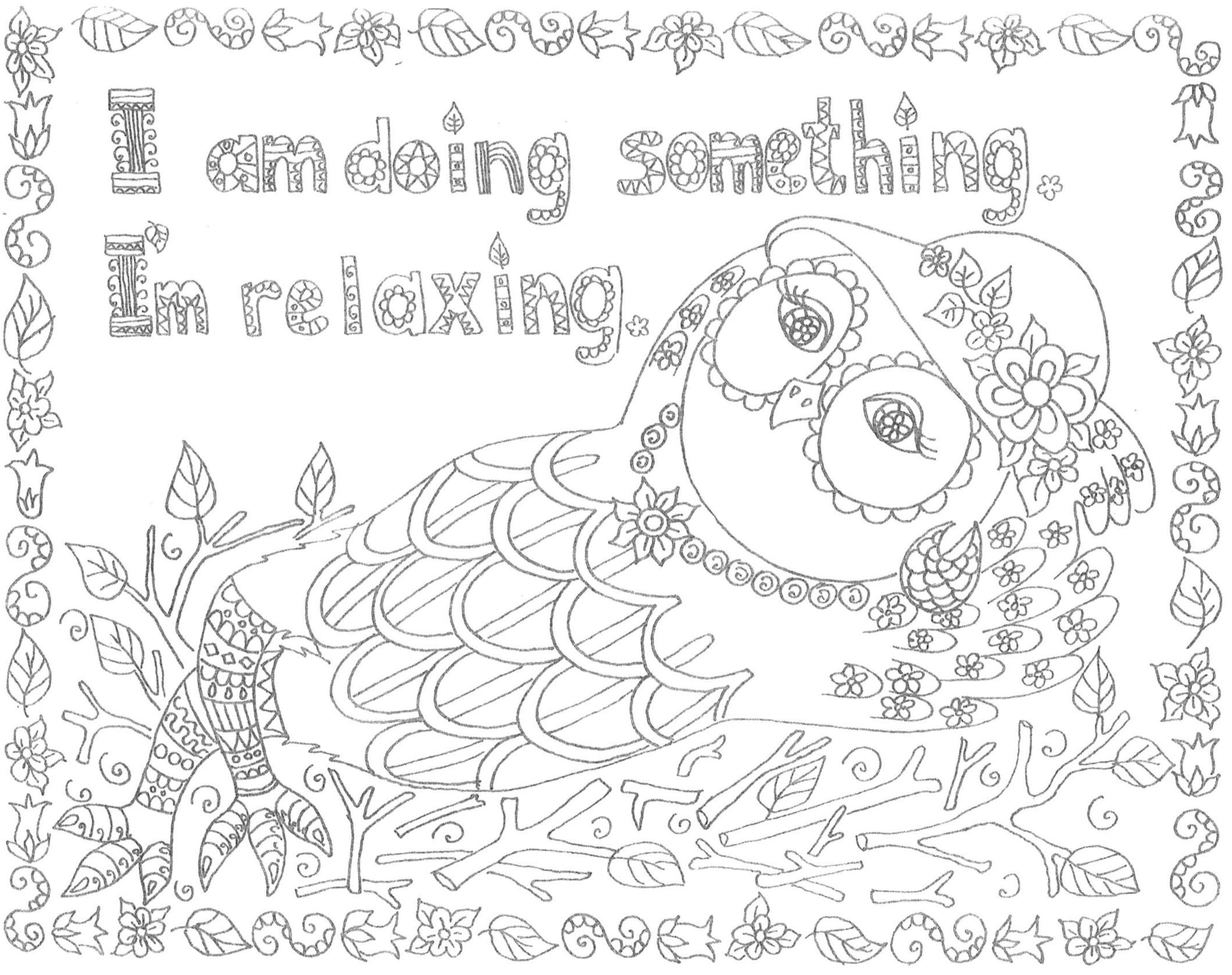
I am doing something.
I'm relaxing.

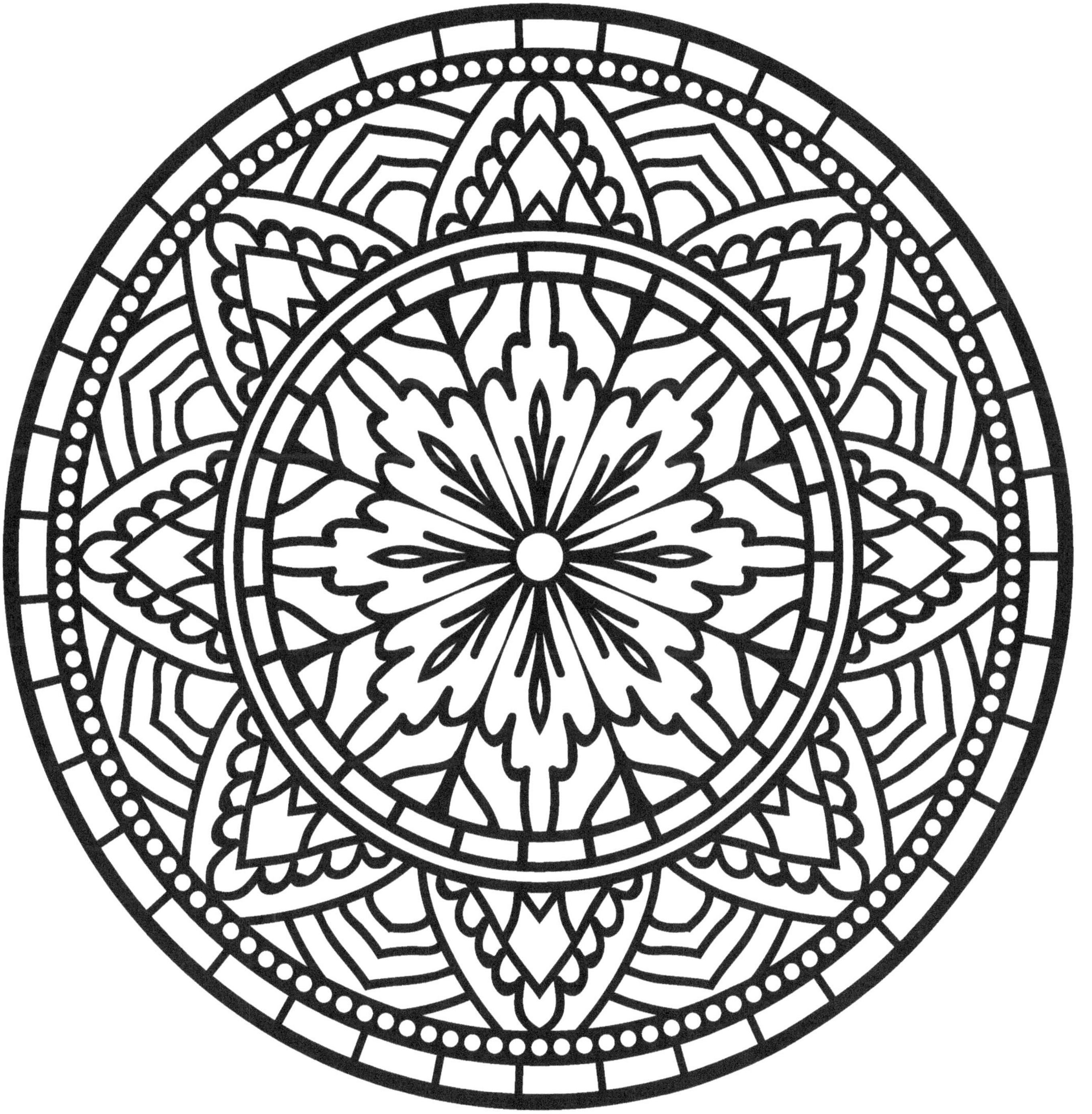

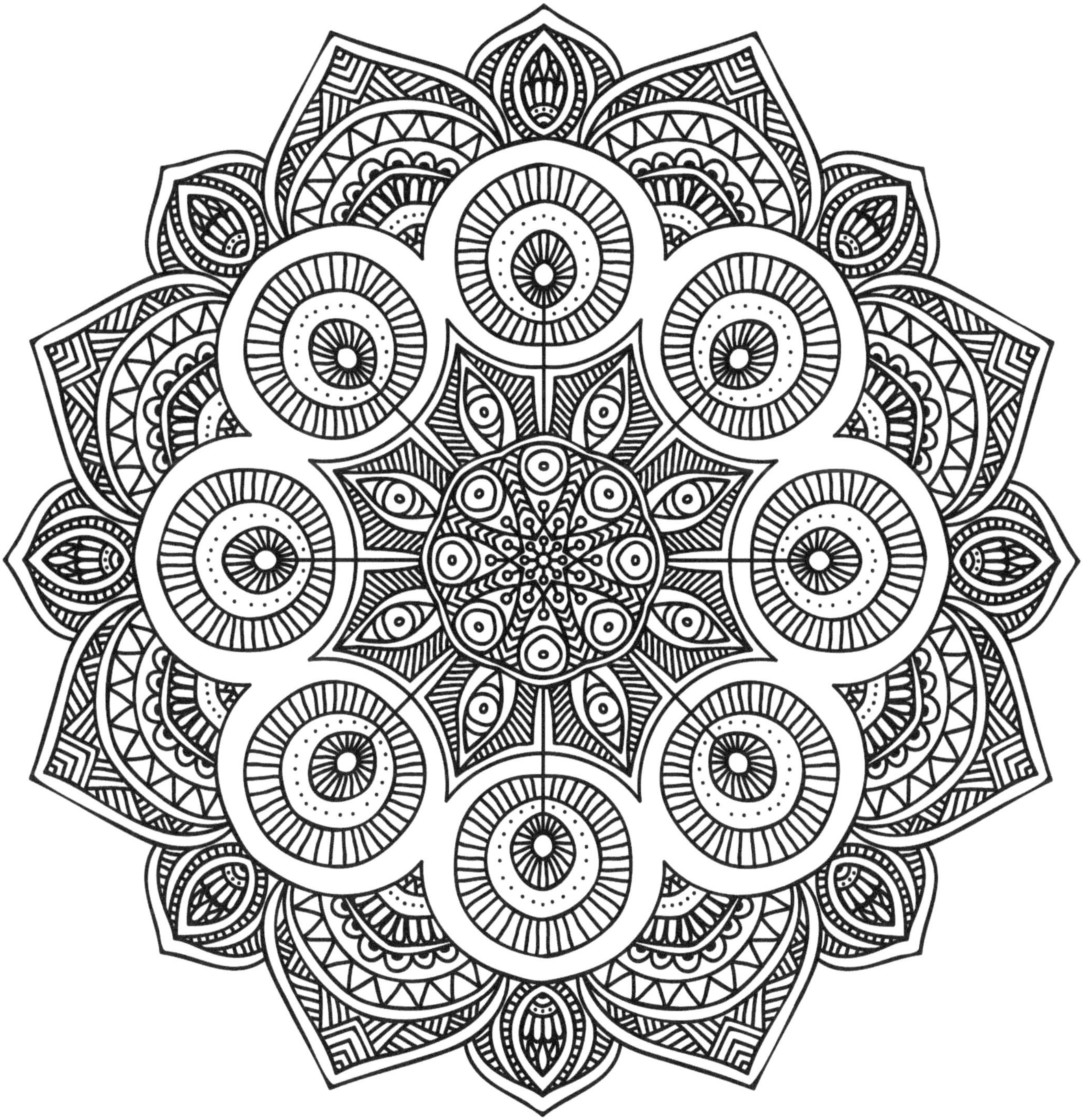

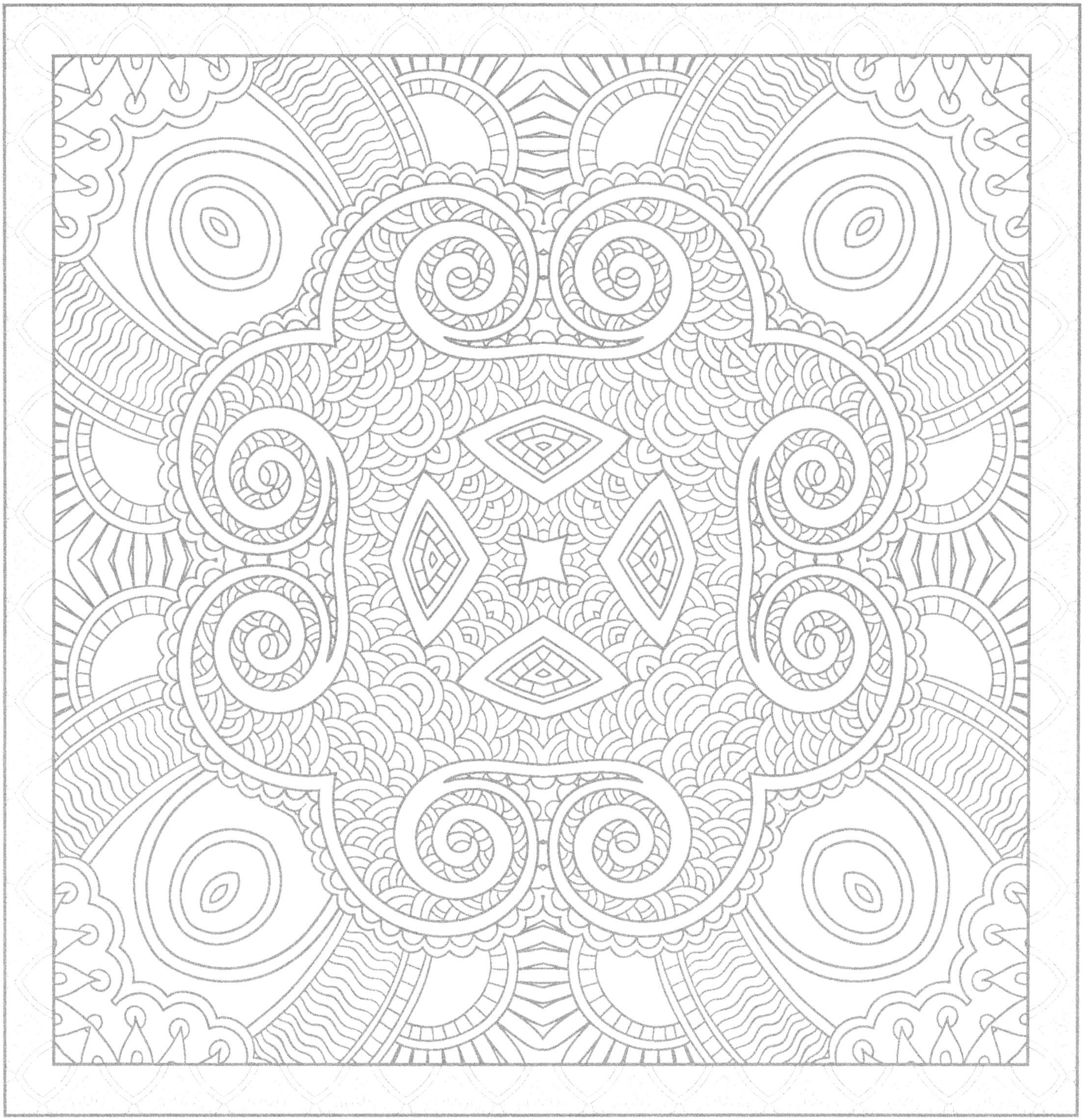

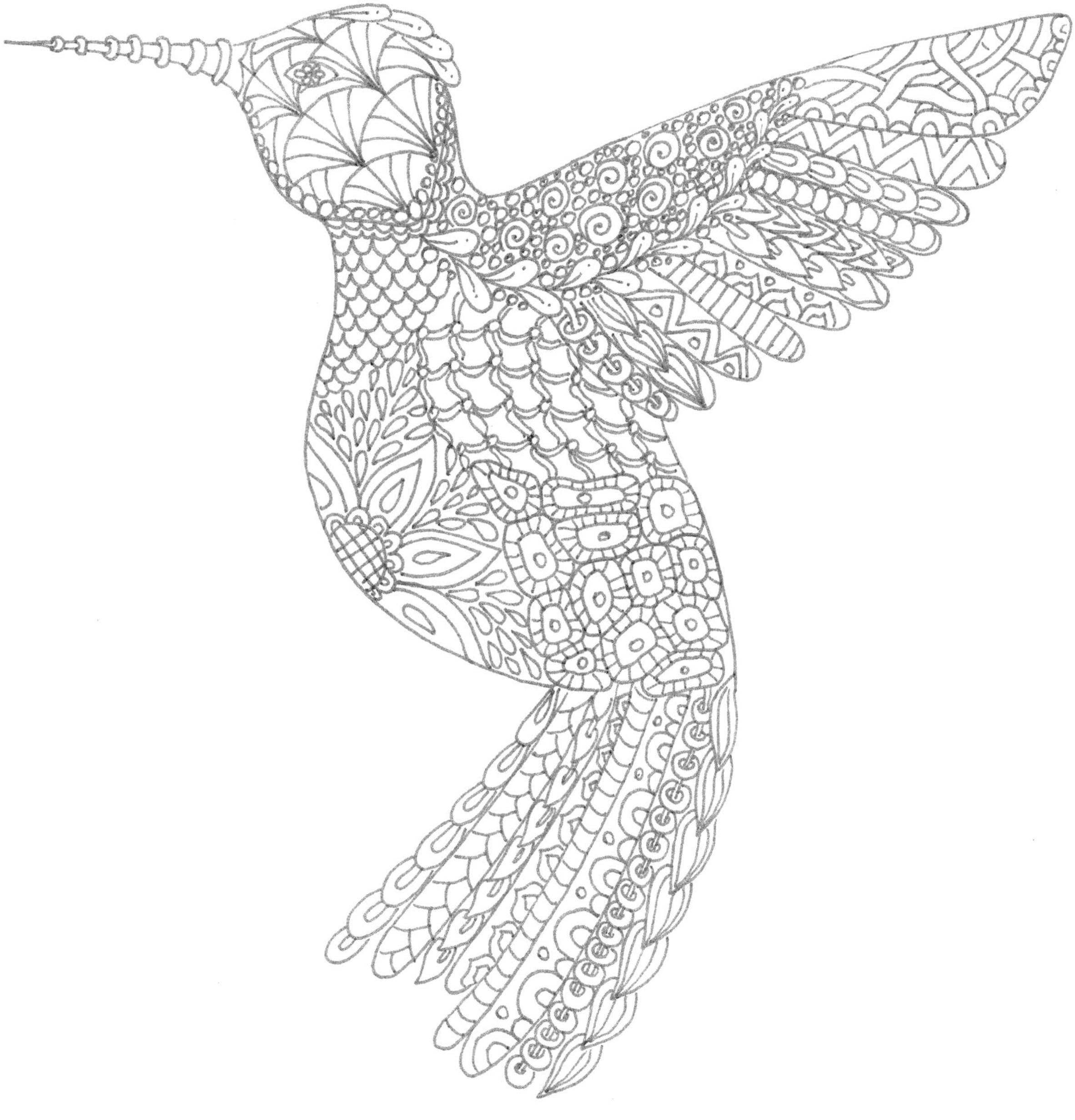

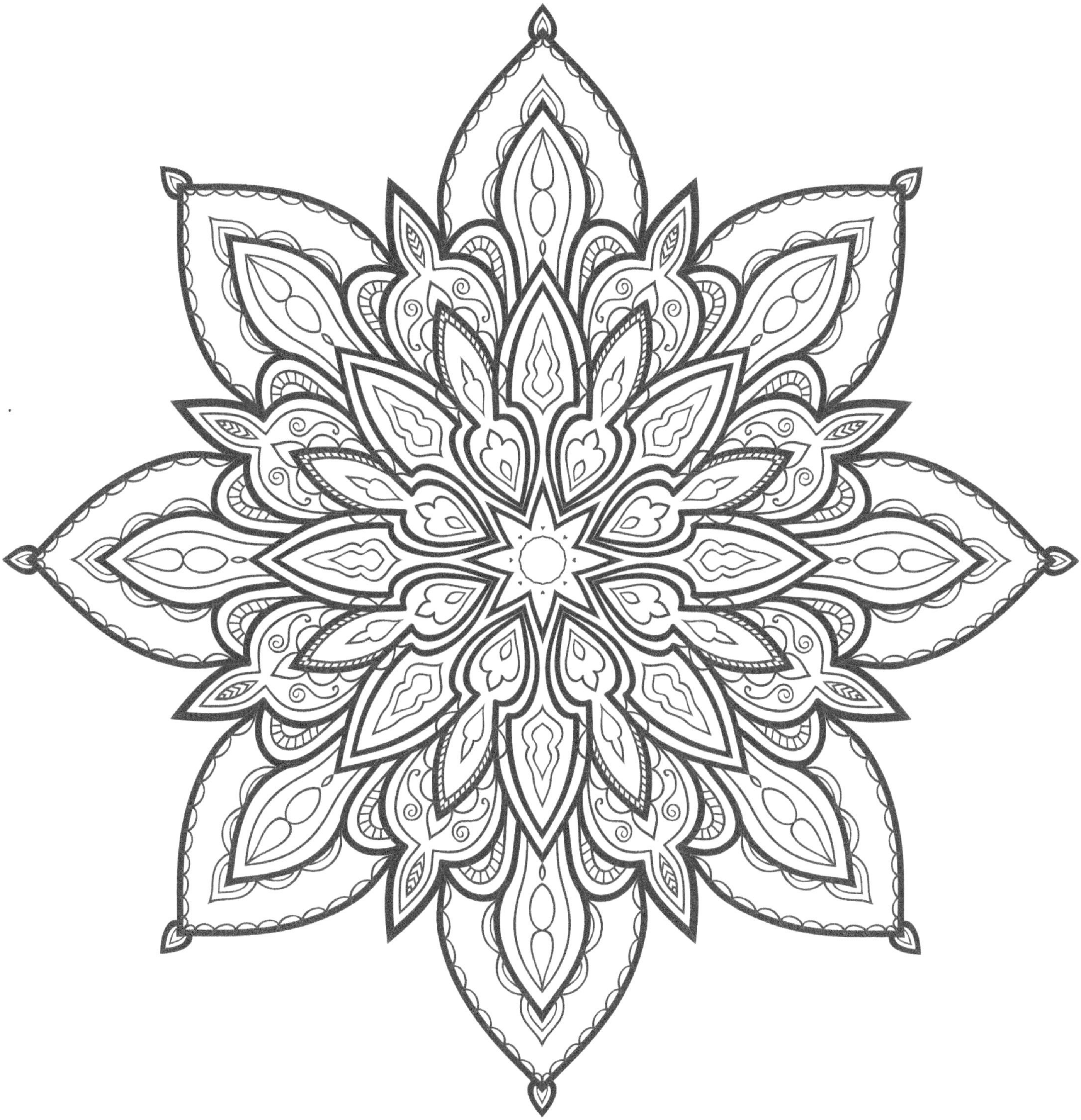

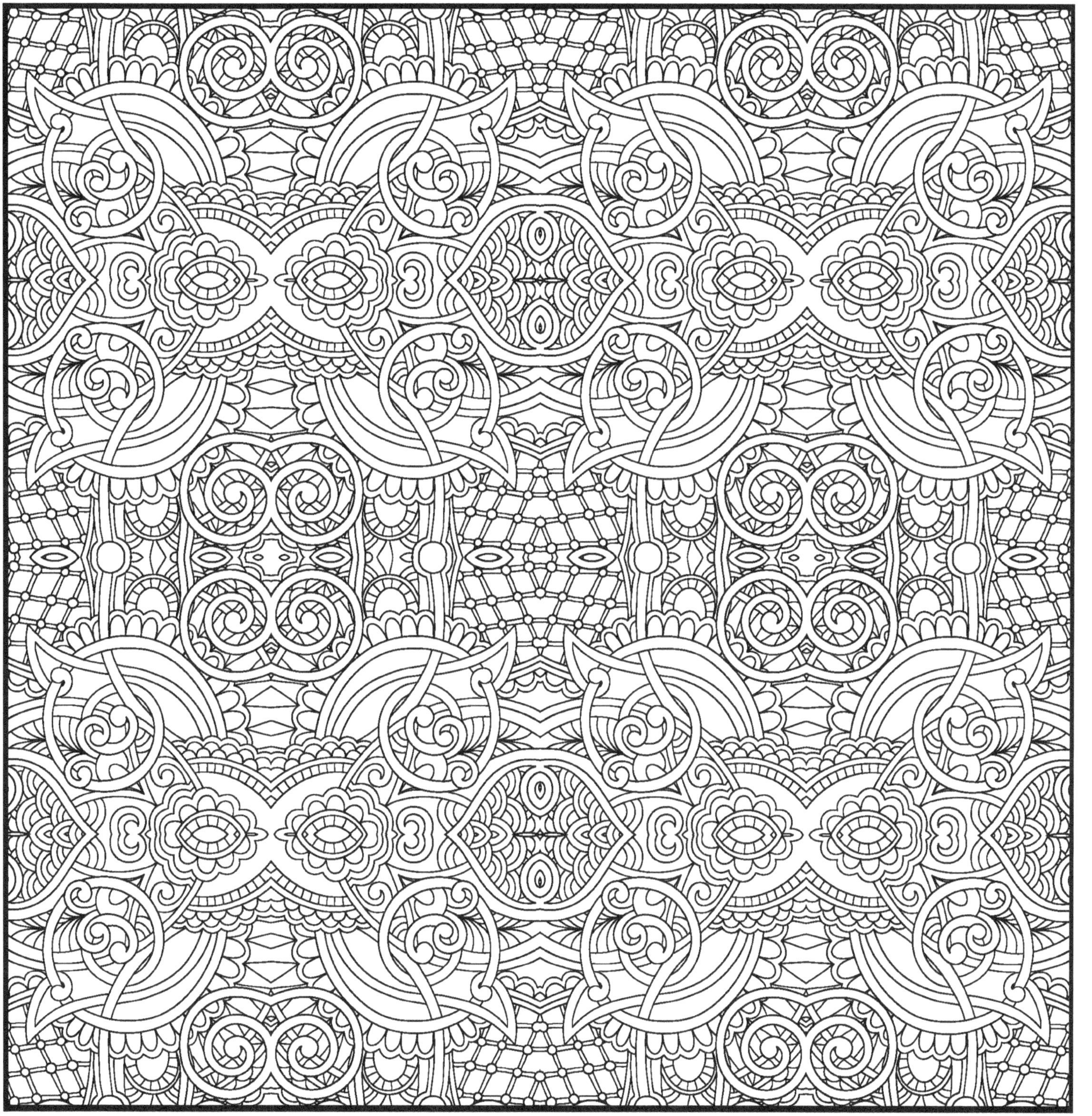

www.ingramcontent.com/pod-product-compliance
Lightning Source LLC
Chambersburg PA
CBHW081509080526
44589CB00017B/2701
9781773800325